CW01221318

MEMOIRS OF A STORE DETECTIVE

MEMOIRS OF A STORE DETECTIVE

Christine Smith

ARTHUR H. STOCKWELL LTD
Torrs Park, Ilfracombe, Devon, EX34 8BA
Established 1898
www.ahstockwell.co.uk

© *Christine Smith, 2013*
First published in Great Britain, 2013
All rights reserved.
*No part of this publication may be reproduced
or transmitted in any form or by any means,
electronic or mechanical, including photocopy,
recording, or any information storage and
retrieval system, without permission
in writing from the copyright holder.*

*British Library Cataloguing-in-Publication Data.
A catalogue record for this book is available
from the British Library.*

*Arthur H. Stockwell Ltd bears no responsibility
for the accuracy of information recorded in this book.*

ISBN 978-0-7223-4323-4
*Printed in Great Britain by
Arthur H. Stockwell Ltd
Torrs Park   Ilfracombe
Devon EX34 8BA*

CONTENTS

How It All Began	7
At the Police Station	15
The Farm Lady	20
Male Shoplifters	27
The Police and Us	38
Women Shoplifters and an Honest VIP	49
Some Who Nearly Got Away	59
Two Particular Shoplifters and the Consequences	71
A New Job	80
New Staff for Me	87
Various Incidents	92
First Aid	112
Someone You Know	120
In Conclusion	122

HOW IT ALL BEGAN

"I am a store detective employed by this store and you have left without paying for some items. Please return with me to the manager's office."

The usual phrase was said outside the store, and my stomach was in my mouth. Would the accused hit me, knife me or run, or had I made a terrible mistake? Perhaps the person had not stolen anything. Desperately I watched the accused person's face; as always it was blank.

Now some words were forming. It was all right.

She said, "I am sorry – I forgot to pay."

My stomach returned to its place and I could breathe again. Calmly I said we must return to the office to discuss it. Once we were inside the store I could feel my legs again, and carefully I guided my thief towards the office. All the staff knew when I had 'got one' because I would be white and always walking very close behind the accused. I needed to keep an eye on her, and to watch she didn't get rid of the item, because if I got her to the office and there were no goods I would have to explain why this innocent woman had been stopped by me.

You'll see I've started by calling the shoplifter 'she', not because I have anything against women, but because out of 300 caught by me only thirty were men. I will give examples of how I caught and dealt with men later.

To continue with the lady now in the office. She was seated, in tears, with one pair of white pants, one pair of pink and one of blue, two pairs of tights and a child's cardigan on the manager's desk.

I relate the facts: "At 11.35 a.m. I saw this lady looking at tights on display. She carefully folded the tights up, and then, holding them in her right hand, she walked away, and whilst doing so dropped them into her shopping bag. She then looked about her and left by the front doors, going out into the main street. It was here I stopped her."

The lady, still in tears, says she did not pay for the other things either. The police are called, and another case is under way. The police collect the lady from the shop. I make a statement in writing at the police station and about two weeks later I have to appear at court with the lady, who is asked whether she is guilty or not guilty. The magistrates hear the evidence and have to come to their conclusion regarding whether she is guilty or not, and decide the punishment, if there is any.

In this case the lady, who was of good previous behaviour, pleaded guilty and was fined £10. The goods were returned to the store and I set off again to catch another one.

My life as a store detective began when my children had started school and I was at a loss for something to do. An advertisement appeared in our local paper: 'Store detective wanted for local departmental store. Experience not necessary as training given. Hours: twenty per week, to suit applicant.' By applying I was not committing myself, so I wrote a nice little letter.

Two days later I received a letter thanking me for my application and saying I would shortly receive further communication. A week later I received a letter asking me to attend for an interview on Thursday 19 December at 2 p.m. I shook. I thought I was daft – I had no experience. Before my marriage I was a trained nanny – who did I think I was, that I could carry off this job of store detective!

My husband said that at least if I went for the interview it would be an outing; I might even get a cup of coffee. So on 19 December I caught the bus into town. I was wearing my best coat, which was eight years old. I didn't wear a hat, but did have high-heeled shoes on. I remember this particularly because the gentleman who showed me round was tall and we raced everywhere and my high heels were a nuisance. However, I arrived at the store and was shown to the staff office by a nice young lady assistant.

The undermanager stuck his head round the door: "You must be Mrs Smith. Would you come in here?"

I followed and he asked questions – what, I can't remember. Then we went for the gallop round the store, eventually landing up at the front entrance. He shook me by the hand and said he would write.

I must have got home somehow, but I don't remember the journey. My husband asked how it had gone, and I said, "No coffee," and that, I thought, was that. After all, I must have appeared quite dumb and useless to the undermanager.

Two days later a white envelope with the firm's own stamp appeared in my letter box. I was sure it would say, 'Thank you for attending the interview, but the post has now been filled.' In fact, I read those words.

My husband, who was calm, read:

Dear Mrs Smith,
    Thank you for attending the interview, we have much pleasure in telling you, you have been selected to the short list and could you call and see us on 22nd December at 11.15 a.m. because on that date the chief security officer will be visiting our branch, if this is not convenient please phone us and we will make alternative arrangements.

I had another cup of coffee and thought, 'Well, getting on the shortlist doesn't mean I've got the job, does it? There are bound to be people with better qualifications than I on the shortlist. I'll go anyway. I might even get a cup of coffee this time.'

So on 22 December 1964, wearing my eight-year-old best coat (I'd been a housewife and mother for twelve years) and this time not so elegant shoes (ones with flat heels), I ventured forth.

I arrived in good time at the store, and this time I went straight to the staff office. I knew what I was doing – ha ha!

When I knocked, the undermanager said, "Come in." In I went and he said, "Ah! Mrs Smith, it's the manager's office you want this time."

This knocked the tiny bit of self-confidence out of me and I followed meekly as a young office girl took me down three flights of stairs, along two corridors, across a yard and up a flight of stairs. Then there was a brown door with the word 'MANAGER' across it. The office girl just pointed and fairly ran away.

'Just what is he like?' I thought. 'If I knock quietly, he might not hear and I can go away.'

I tapped very gently and a woman's voice snapped, "Come in."

I twisted the handle and there sat a woman in her late thirties surrounded by filing cabinets and papers and typewriters.

"Oh," she said, "Mrs Smith?"

I nodded (I'd left my voice somewhere).

"The undermanager rang through and said you were on your way," she continued. "The manager won't be long."

She returned to her typing, and I stood for about three minutes.

Then the door to the left of her opened, and a giant of a man bellowed, "Mrs Smith." It was a Father Christmas sort of bellow, very friendly.

I relaxed a little and followed him into his office. He showed me to a chair. I sat. He spoke about the job and asked what I would do if my children were ill and during the school holidays. I said, "I have a good neighbour, so all would be well if they were ill, and she would cope with the holidays."

Then the original man in a raincoat came in. This, I was informed, was the chief security officer. We shook hands.

He looked me over and then said to the manager, "Well, there's nothing noticeable about her." The manager went red and glared at the security officer, who turned to me and said, "It's yours – the job, I mean. Can you start after Christmas – two weeks' paid training at our head office."

I said, "I can start the day the children go back to school, January the 10th."

He said, "Fine. I'll see you in my office." He said goodbye to the manager and strode out of the office.

The manager stood up and said, "Our security officer is a good detective, but I'm afraid – and I do apologise for him – he lacks manners." He continued: "I will be in touch with you. Thank you for coming."

I stood up on what appeared to be two pieces of wood instead of legs and then I left the office. I came out of the office into a corridor and then found a door which led into the shop.

'Well,' I thought, 'if I am going to be the store detective here, I'll have a quiet look around.'

I ambled around, and no one took any notice of me. I felt as though I had a large notice across my head saying, 'I'm going to be your new store detective.' I don't know now whether I was delighted I'd got the job because it proved to me I wasn't just a housewife or because I would soon be earning money, or because it showed that I was actually better than someone else for this particular job. Anyway, I went to the store's self-service restaurant and had a cup of coffee – the first one I had had in a café for about eight years.

I enjoyed that coffee and then went home. I phoned my husband and he was delighted.

We all enjoyed Christmas, and then on 5 January I received a letter with train tickets and directions telling me how to get to the security office in London.

I now considered that I was in need of psychiatric help. Who in their right mind would have applied for the job of store detective?

10 January 1965 dawned. I had got myself an au pair, and she got the children to school and enabled me to get to the station on time. I took a taxi. I was early. "I think I'll go home. No, you won't." This tussle was going on inside me.

The train eventually arrived. Amazingly, I got in. We were off. I sat rigid during the whole of the two-hour journey. The train arrived. I got out and took a taxi. I felt dreadful.

I got to the office and was warmly greeted. Training began. For two weeks, every day, I went. Soon it all came to an end. I was trained, but not free to act as a store detective in my own branch until I had got to know the layout and staff.

I wandered around the store, and for two weeks I saw nothing happen at all. I learnt that the previous store detective had caught one shoplifter in two years. I began to wonder if I could walk about in the store without catching anyone, or would I go potty? I got some very funny looks from various members of the selling staff. I, of course, had not been introduced to them because I was just supposed to be a customer.

Many times I was approached by a sales assistant, who said, "Can I help you, madam?" To which I replied, "No, thank you – I'm only looking."

Eventually I was called into the manager's office. His secretary was most helpful, now that I knew her better.

I was ushered into the office and sat opposite the manager, who said, "Now, Mrs Smith, you have been with us for one whole month. Your general behaviour is good, and I now propose to allow you to act as our store detective. Be careful and good luck."

I wandered away from the office, thinking, 'For two weeks I've seen nothing. I don't suppose I ever will see anything.' Anyway, less than one hour later I was in the office with my very first shoplifter.

I was in the jumper and skirt department when one of the staff, who was alert and by this time knew who I was, came up to me and said, pointing to a particular woman, "That woman, I'm sure, pinched a skirt about six weeks ago."

My ears pricked up. Here at last was a genuine shoplifter. I followed her to every department and eventually we found ourselves in the lighting department. I had almost given up and thought the assistant was mistaken. My legs were extremely wobbly and my heart was pounding with fear. The woman looked about her and then picked up a table lamp – a wooden one, about eighteen inches high. She looked at it, looked about her and then – replaced it. I felt as though there was a steel band around my head, tightening. The woman walked away into other departments; I followed, just in case. All the time I was trying to appear like a normal customer. Just a minute! Mrs A (as I shall call her from now on) was undoing her overcoat buttons. It wasn't particularly warm. Again my interest picked up. What now? She stood for a short while and then returned to the lighting department. She stood at the entrance to the department, shrugging her coat back a bit over her shoulders. I was not far behind her. We entered the department almost together. She went straight to the table lamp, picked it up and tucked it into her coat. She drew her coat over it and then walked away.

'Come on, legs – move.' My shoes felt as if they were suddenly cemented to the ground.

Anyway, as she moved off I managed to follow. She quickly went out of the store, and as she got past the frontage of the shop I touched her arm and said, "Excuse me. I am a store detective and you have left without paying for a table lamp." Mrs A said nothing and I continued: "Please come with me to the manager's office."

She had gone a horrid grey colour. My goodness, I had no experience of first aid. Would she pass out or even pass on? What had I done? What a ghastly job, hurting people this way! Whatever was I talking about? Mrs A was the one who had done wrong, not me. The wretched woman had stolen a table lamp and we were now on our way to the office.

We arrived, and went in through the door marked 'MANAGER', Mrs A still with the table lamp under her coat. It was quite amazing. The secretary jumped up from her seat and went straight into the manager's office. Two people came out of his office and we were ushered in. Mrs A sat in a chair opposite the manager.

I stood and said, "At 11.45 a.m. I received information that this lady is suspected of shoplifting a short while ago, and I have kept her under observation while she was in the shop. In the lighting department I saw her take a table lamp from the display, place it inside her coat and leave without paying for it. Outside the shop I stopped her and told her who I am and brought her back to the office."

The manager then spoke to Mrs A: "Well?" he said. "And what have you to say?"

Mrs A said, as she put the table lamp on the desk, "I don't know why I did it. I've not been well – I've been on some pills."

The manager looked at me and nodded. I went out of the office and phoned for the police to come. I returned to the office and we waited. Eventually the police arrived. I repeated the facts.

One of the policewomen then turned to Mrs A and said, "You

are not obliged to say anything; but if you do, it may be taken down and given in evidence. Why did you do it?"

Mrs A said, "I've been under the doctor."

The policewoman then said, "Come on – let's get it sorted out at the police station."

Off they all went and took the table lamp with them. I was to follow in about half an hour.

After they had gone the manager looked at me and said with a broad grin, "Well done! Now we'll have some more."

I had a drink of water then went off to the police station.

AT THE POLICE STATION

I arrived, breathless from nerves and running, at the local cop shop. I went up to a dark-brown wooden partition with 'Enquiries' written above a frosted pane of glass. I gently knocked on this frosted glass.

It shot straight up and a frosty police sergeant with a heard-it-all-before look on his face said, "Yes?"

I was in the land of professional thief-catchers.

I said, "I'm Mrs Smith from the store. I caught a shoplifter and your police officers told me to come here and make a statement."

I paused and the Sergeant said, "Male or female?" I must have looked dreadfully dumb because he bellowed, "The shoplifter."

"Oh," said I, regaining my timid voice, "female."

The Sergeant continued: "Uniform or plain clothes?" Again my dumb look must have reappeared because oh, so patiently he said, "The police officers."

I said, "Oh, plain clothes."

He smilingly said, "You want the CID upstairs," and he promptly dropped his window.

I was left standing utterly alone in a dark hall with many doors leading off it. There was no proper ceiling, just a circular window high up in the roof. Hanging from this on a long, long chain was a sort of chandelier, but only one bulb was working. The Sergeant had said "upstairs", but did I grab the chandelier and hope it was a lift? There was obviously an upstairs, but how did one get there?

I took a deep breath and thought, 'I'm a sort of detective; I must detect where the stairs are.'

Opposite 'Enquiries' was an arch which looked interesting, so I walked over to it. Through it I saw a covered yard with police cars all waiting for the next crime to be reported. Then they would be away to find the culprits – with their police officers, of course. I stood for a few moments under the arch and then I saw to my right, tucked neatly in a corner, an iron staircase which led up to a door with 'CID' written in chalk or paint. I don't know to this day which, because as I was just about to run a damp finger over the letters the door was pulled open and I fell in.

A rather large, grey-haired, motherly lady said, "Did you want something, dear?"

I felt most 'humilified' – me, the wonder store detective, flat on my face, half in and half out of the room marked 'CID'.

I struggled up and said, "I'm the store detective from the store and I caught a shoplifter female. She was brought here by plain-clothes police officers who said I was to come and make a statement."

"Oh," she said, "we've not met. I'm WDC —. How did you get in here?"

I said, "The man at the window marked 'Enquiries' said I had to go upstairs, and these were the only ones I could find.

WDC — said, "He's been told we can't have just anybody walking about all over the police station. He should have phoned us and we'd have come and got you. Wait here." And she raced off down the stairs.

While doing as I was told, waiting, I began to think over what had been happening. Nothing had made me feel the way I had thought I'd feel when I caught a shoplifter. I was being made to feel as though I was the one who had done wrong. I'd had to walk three-quarters of a mile to the police station, whereas the shoplifter had gone by car. I'd had to find the stairs, and then I'd been told, "We can't just have anybody walking about the police station."

Well, here came WDC — up the stairs, and I sort of followed her as she hurtled past me, through another door, into a large room with eight big desks and green-and-cream walls (bottom half green, top half cream). In one corner sat the shoplifter and she was having her photo taken for the bad book. I was shown to a seat by a nice young police lady, who I found out was called Sue. She sat opposite me, took some papers from a drawer and borrowed a cigarette from a male police officer who happened to be seated at another desk, and we began. I related the exact facts of the case, and she wrote, occasionally asking me how to spell various words.

After about a quarter of an hour, when we were very nearly finished, the door absolutely flew open and banged against the wall.

I jumped out of my chair, but Sue sat very composedly and said, "What did you say?"

At the same moment a young lad of about sixteen years of age burst in, swearing. He said, "Lousy - - - - coppers! You were waiting for us. Who's the grass? I'll make sure he grows green when I find him."

Two charming plain-clothes police officers followed the lad in and plonked him in the chair vacated by my shoplifter when her photos had been taken.

Sue handed me my statement, saying, "Read and then sign it, please."

I read and signed it, and was taken to the door and shown the way out.

Later, through our local paper, I learnt that the lad had been caught forcing his way into the sports pavilion of a local factory. His friend had been able to run quicker than him, and the lad never did say what his friend's name was. He got put on probation for two years by the local magistrates' court. Although that's got nothing to do with me, I'd hate you to be for ever wondering what dark deeds the lad had been up to. Now we all know.

Three months later my lady shoplifter was called before the local magistrates. She pleaded guilty and was fined £15.

The shoplifter appeared to have been treated better than I was. Later, when I became one of the regular recognized detectives, I found out what does go on in the police station when a shoplifter is caught; and, later still, I found out that the procedure varies from area to area.

Mrs A did go to the police station in the police car, but she was quite ashamed of the fact. You see, she had had to walk through the shop to the main entrance with a police officer in front of her and one behind. I know they weren't in uniform, but there is something about a police officer that tells you instinctively that he or she is one (a police officer, I mean). After being shepherded through the shop, Mrs A had to get into the back of the panda car – and have you ever noticed that whenever people see a police car they just stand around hoping to catch a glimpse of whatever trouble is going on. Anyway, with Mrs A in the back of the car, the police officers in the front and the table lamp safely in the hands of the policewoman, they were on their way.

At the police station they drove straight into the covered yard. They took Mrs A up the stairs to the CID, so she was spared the gapes from passers-by that end – no one who works there takes much notice anyway. They've seen it all before.

To continue Mrs A's journey, she was taken to the charge room and officially charged with the offence that took place at our store. She was asked if there was anything she might like to say, and it was written down on a proper statement form. Then she read it through and signed it. This would have been read out in court. A statement gives the magistrates a good idea of the offender's feelings at the time of the offence. Mrs A might have been very muddled due to worry or pills, and this would show in the statement. On the other hand, she might have known exactly what she was doing – that she actually intended to steal, and was being careful not to be caught in the act. In fact, it was such a shock when the hand came on to her shoulder that she confessed in her statement that she had stolen the item. Sometimes when a shoplifter gets home she completely changes her story. She has had time to recover and rethink her excuses, but in court the magistrates will have an account of the happening written by her quite soon after the event. One of the most degrading things that happens during the visit to the police station is that all the shoplifter's goods are examined. Her handbag and other bags are looked through. The amount of money she is carrying is noted. Her pockets are searched, and sometimes a complete body search is carried out – but not in this case. With Mrs A, just her belongings and pockets were searched. She was carrying a lot of money – £46 2s. 6d. – so there appeared to be no reason for her to steal the table lamp. As I said, procedures vary from station to station. The next item on Mrs A's agenda was a visit to the fingerprint man. He took each of her fingers separately, pressed them on an ink pad and then printed them on a special card.

She then washed her hands to get rid of the ink. Then it was off to the police photographer, who took her photo for the records – one from the front, and one from each side.

You know, it really is quite awful; and it's not until some shoplifters get to the police station and all these rather nasty happenings take place, that the shoplifter realizes the severity of the thing she has done. For years I've said 'shoplifting' is the wrong name for the crime, because crime it is. Many shoplifters don't realize until they are caught that they are stealing and they will be charged with theft. How many of these people would dream of stealing anything anywhere else? I think notices in shops should read, 'Shoplifting is stealing and stealing is a crime', instead of the usual notices saying shoplifters will be prosecuted. When a person is found guilty at a magistrates' court they have a criminal record. Many people, particularly women, realize too late what they have been actually doing. As I said before, they are really stealing. Lots of 'well-off' ladies find it a game to take something from a shop without paying. It is a bit of a thrill to outwit the shop staff, including, if there is one, the store detective. They are very careful not to be seen by anyone, and it comes to them too late that the store detective has actually seen them after all. The detective has quite a lot of advantages: she knows where she can best observe a department without being actually in it, she has all the staff on her side (after all, the more stuff goes missing, the less bonus the staff get), there are aides like two-way mirrors and, nowadays, closed-circuit TV. A thief may get away with it on a couple of occasions, but there will come a time, as happened with Mrs A, when he or she is caught.

Mrs A's poor husband was horrified. He arrived at the police station after I had left, to take Mrs A home, and I heard later from Sue that he kept saying to Mrs A, "Why? You have enough money. I'd have got that blasted lamp if you wanted it. You've got your chequebook. Why? Why? Why?"

She admitted that she was very bored at home. The children had left home and had families of their own and it was a bit of excitement to be smarter than the store's staff, and to actually take something from a shelf or hanger and not be seen. It made her day – it was so exciting.

THE FARM LADY

Apart from my daily duties of looking for and occasionally finding shoplifters, after I had been with the firm about six months they decided to further my duties to include watching for stolen cheques, and fraudulent deals concerned with cash and accounts.

At our store they have an account system whereby a customer who has opened an account with the credit department, can go to any department and for any item less then £10 say to the assistant, "I'll have it on my account." The assistant then writes out a bill, and the customer gives her name and address and signs the bill. The goods are then wrapped up and the customer takes her goods. At the end of the month an account is sent to her and she pays for all items on her bill. This is convenient for many customers. I used to call it my 'free shop', because before I worked there I had an account and even if it was the middle of the month and I had no money I could still have items. However, the end of the month wasn't so good, when the bills came in. I always managed to get up early towards the end of the month, when the bill was due, because then I could meet the postman and carefully remove the store envelope before my husband saw it. Then when he had had his breakfast, and was ready for the day, I would carefully return it to the mat as though the postman had forgotten it on his first delivery. If my lord and master was in a bad mood, the bill waited a day or two.

I expect you are wondering why I've named this chapter 'The Farm Lady' and I'm rabbiting on about shop accounts and how I deal with bills coming to our house. Without further delay I'll proceed.

As I have said, to get items all a customer had to do was give her name and address and sign her name. It was about the middle of the month when the credit manager called me to his office and explained that he had received two bills marked 'NOT KNOWN' and 'ADDRESS DOES NOT EXIST', returned from the post office. They had been sent to two separate people at two separate farm addresses. The first was for two pairs of sheets purchased on 3 August 1964 by a Mrs Gibbs of — Farm at a village five miles from the town; the second was for four pairs of tights and one pair of gloves, purchased on the same date, this time by Mrs Parrish of — Farm at another village, again about five miles from the town. The credit manager and I thought the assistants in both cases had not written the names and addresses properly, and so we questioned the girls. Both were unable to give any information because it was about six weeks since the customers were in. They just couldn't remember anything at all.

I was instructed to keep my eyes open when customers were making purchases by account, just in case. Nothing happened, except that I caught two more shoplifters. Then I received another call to go to the credit manager's office. Again it was the middle of the month, and I just wondered.

"Ah!" he said. "We have another farm."

The bill had been returned from the post office with 'ADDRESS DOES NOT EXIST' written across it. This time it had been addressed to Mrs Gray, — Farm at another village, again situated five miles from the town. The items 'purchased' were from the children's department, valued at £9 15s. Because it had been less than £10 no questions were asked at the time of the purchase, apart from the usual name and address. The credit manager and I went to see the assistant in the children's department and showed her the copy of the bill she had made out for the customer. We asked her if she could remember anything about the purchase.

She thought for a few minutes and then said, "You know, I can remember her. I'm sure it was the woman who asked if we delivered small goods. She had bought children's socks, a small-sized dress and a leotard for her seven-year-old daughter. While I was making out the bill she said, 'I wonder would you deliver them to me?' I looked up our delivery-van list, and said, 'The van to your village doesn't come out till Thursday of next week.' It was Friday, so the woman said, 'Oh, don't bother – I'll take them.' She signed 'A. Gray' and left with the things. I thought at the time it was odd because it was only a small parcel."

Delighted with this information, I got out my pen and notebook and said to the assistant, "Describe her to me."

Silence. The assistant then said, "You know, I can't remember her appearance at all."

We'd drawn a blank. We tried to help the assistant remember – was the woman dark, fair, tall, short, fat or thin? It was no use. She just couldn't remember anything other than the conversation about delivery.

The credit manager and I returned to his office to discuss the problem. We came to the conclusion that we were being done, and we sent a note to every department stating that an unknown person was obtaining goods and giving fictitious names and addresses. The address usually was a farm in a village in the locality. If an assistant should be given a suspicious name and address, she was to engage the customer in conversation and send for me or the manager. We also asked the staff to be vigilant. This was all we could do.

Another month passed. Again we were in the middle of the month when I received another request to see the credit manager, who showed me another returned bill: Mrs Clayton, — Farm at another village. The shop probably doesn't want everyone to know they were taken for a ride so I can't name the villages. Incidentally, it can't happen now because every account customer has his or her own account card, very similar to an Access card or Barclaycard, and no purchase can be made without this card. Anyway, the credit manager and I visited the assistant who had 'sold' Mrs Clayton an iron for £8 14s. She could remember nothing about the transaction. We did remind her that she had had instructions not to let anyone have items on account when a farm was given in the address without checking with me or the manager.

Very haughtily she replied, "I only started three weeks ago and no one told me."

The farm lady knew what she was up to, didn't she?

Four weeks later, I visited the credit manager. It was now four months since the start of this business. Yes, there it was: an account returned 'NOT KNOWN' from Mrs Hedge, The Park, — village. She had us on a piece of string. Mrs Hedge, The Park! I ask you! This time she had 'bought' cosmetics to the value of £9 2s. 6d. I went to the assistant on cosmetics and said, "It's happened again. The farm lady has struck and this time it's your department."

"Oh no," said the assistant on cosmetics, "I've sold nothing to a farm address. I've been most careful. Once I was a little concerned – a lady of about forty-five years, 5 feet 8 inches tall, wearing a hat and dark glasses. She had a very scarred complexion with darkish and greasy heavy eyebrows. She gave her address as . . . wait a minute," she said. "I've got an order for her – a special cream I've ordered for her bad complexion. Actually I've got her address here." She brought out her special order book, and she read, "Mrs Hedge, The Park." The assistant, on seeing my face, said, "Oh, no, it's not her. It can't be. There's no farm in the address."

I nodded and said it was her. We went over the description again.

The assistant said, "Well, I'll know her when she comes to collect her cream."

I felt like saying, "She won't come to you again," but I did say, "Well, let me know when she calls."

Needless to say, the cream never was collected.

Again in the middle of the next month another letter was returned 'NOT KNOWN': Mrs Watts, — Farm. She had 'purchased' this time two bras, two vests and six pairs of pants for £9 19s. The farm lady must have known about the £10 limit, because everything she bought was a little less than the maximum £10.

I spoke to the assistant who had served her. By now I was feeling most inadequate. Why couldn't she be found out? The cost of the goods she had had amounted to £51 10s. 6d.

The assistant looked at the copy of the bill and said, "I do think I remember this customer. She was quite small. The bras were size 32, as you see here on the bill. I seem to remember she was possibly aged about twenty-two and she had fair hair – oh yes, and long red fingernails."

Now we had two descriptions. I asked the assistant why she thought she remembered the customer and why she hadn't informed the manager or me when serving the customer.

"Oh," she said, "the reason I remember her is because when she gave her address as a farm I wondered if she might be the farm lady, but she was so nice, and she was telling me about her daughter's pony, which was expecting at any time, that I thought she couldn't be a crook; so I didn't bother, but I do remember what she looks like."

I quickly left the assistant because I felt like calling her all the names under the sun, and that was certainly not done at our store. The credit manager and I, five months on and over £50 poorer, could find no way of catching this lady!

Two more mid-month visits to the credit office provided two more fictitious names and addresses (Mrs Hodge, — Farm and Mrs Ballard, — Farm). Goods to the value of £18 17s. 6d., consisting of a china tea set and a hairdryer, had been taken and the staff concerned could give us no further information.

It was now April. For ten months the farm lady had been making her one 'purchase' a month, each worth approximately £9. We'd examined the signatures on the bills, we'd gone through all the accounts of customers with real farm addresses, we'd nagged and nagged the staff, and we had got nowhere at all.

I talked to the local crime prevention officer, who was unable to help – all he said was, "Well, get the assistant who serves her to catch her." It was so easy to say, but so very difficult to get the staff to realize that the woman appeared to be just an ordinary shopper. She just wasn't what they expected: a furtive, shifty-eyed crook.

On 4 May our luck sort of changed. It was a bright sunny day and I was in the jumper department. There were not many customers about – just a slight sprinkling of foreign students (who often think shoplifting is fair game). I had been observing two dark-haired Spanish-type girls rummaging through a stand of short-sleeved jumpers. I saw a woman standing at the counter waiting to be served; another lady joined her. The first woman had bad skin and wore glasses; the second woman was small with fair hair. I wondered, but that was all. I saw one of the Spanish girls look about her, then into her bag she dropped a pink short-sleeved jumper. The second Spanish girl, who was on the other side of the stand, picked up a black jumper and that went into her shopping bag. Both girls left the department and went into the ladies' room. I followed them. They did their hair, put some more lipstick on and then left the ladies' room, went down the stairs and out of the front door. I followed them.

When they were beyond the frontage of the shop I caught the arm of one of the girls and said, "I'm a store detective and you've not paid for the jumpers. Do you understand English?"

"Eh?" Jabber, jabber – they didn't understand. "No speak English."

I said, "Come."

They started to walk away from me and the shop. I grabbed one of the girls' arms and as she turned she threw her shopping bag and it fell at the feet of the two ladies who had been in the jumper department.

I said, in between wrestling with the Spanish girls, "I'm a store detective. Please bring this girl's bag into the store for me.

The fair woman, who was carrying her purchase from the jumper department, picked up the Spanish girl's bag and followed me to the manager's office; the second Spanish girl had run off. The woman handed the bag to the manager's secretary and left the shop. I explained to the manager what had happened. The police were called. They came and got the second Spanish girl's name and address from the one in the office, and off they went to the police station.

Just after they had gone and I was recovering there was a timid knock on the office door. The manager boomed, "Come in," and in came the assistant from the jumper department, holding an account bill copy. She was shaking and very, very pale.

She coughed and said, "I think I've served the farm lady. The name and address is Mrs Kent, — Farm, — village. She was with another lady, so I didn't think it was her. I showed my department manager after the two women had gone, just in case, and she said I was to bring it to you."

We rushed to the credit manager's office, where we looked up all farm addresses and also addresses for a Mrs Kent, but nowhere could we find any account for Mrs Kent, — Farm. It was the farm lady. Now could the assistant give a description of the woman? It was one of the women I had wondered about before the two Spanish girls had taken my attention. The fair-haired woman who had helped pick up the Spanish girl's bag and was so cool was probably an accomplice and had been the woman who had the underwear. No wonder we had had two different descriptions!

They were sensible and lucky: we never saw an account made out for a fictitious address again. In fact, I never saw either of them again. I had spoiled the chance of catching them by the fracas with the Spanish girls, but we lost no more money through fictitious accounts. I really don't know who won, them or us, but I'll always remember the farm ladies.

MALE SHOPLIFTERS

After catching my first shoplifter, the day I was given permission to catch them all by myself, over the next six years I apprehended over 300 persons. The majority were female, but I would like to devote this chapter to some of the men I caught, and also those who got away. As I said at the beginning, I had training at Head Office and regularly an experienced store detective came and spent a day with me, talking over any problems I had. The greatest joy of her coming was that she always took me out to a slap-up lunch somewhere in town. Her third trip to see me was on a Wednesday, and it was fairly quiet. I must have been with the firm for about four months, and had not yet apprehended a man.

Mrs Brown, the store detective from Head Office, said, "Let's get a man."

This sounded OK to me – oh, I see: yes, she meant apprehend a male shoplifter.

We had coffee at ten forty-five and wandered back to the menswear department – really the most suitable place to find a man. Two middle-aged ladies were discussing the benefits of cotton pyjamas for Fred, as against nylon.

"He sweats," said one.

The other laughed and quietly said, "Nylon might cause sparks."

Again they laughed.

"When I buy pyjamas for my husband I always buy a pair similar to the ones I am throwing out."

Perhaps as one gets to be middle-aged one has thoughts about pyjamas. Oh well, I would be middle-aged one day, and then

I'd know what it's all about.

As you can see, being a store detective is not all excitement. Many, many hours are spent just wandering among honest shoppers – because the majority of shoppers are honest. It is only very few who decide to have something and not pay for it, and even then the store detective has to be very near the shopper to know what's going on. Maybe while we were wandering in the menswear department someone was pinching hardware or linens elsewhere in the shop.

The two ladies made their purchases and paid cash and left the department. The time was now eleven forty-five. I stopped and spoke to an assistant about the plants he was always on about. Yes, they were just about ready to start having the tops nipped out. This would make . . .

Mrs Brown came up behind me and said, "Lucy, do look at these shirts. I really think one in blue would be a nice gift."

I thought she had flipped her lid – after all, my name is not Lucy and who wants a gift of a shirt? I turned towards her and, as I did so, she winked at me and her eyes shot over to a young man who had just entered the department. I followed her glance and saw he was carrying a large brown holdall.

I said, "Do you think blue is the right colour?" and together we wandered over to the display of shirts.

To enable Mrs Brown to watch the young man I stood with my back to him and she watched over my shoulder while we were both pretending to look at shirts. The young man had stopped and was looking at the display of sports jackets. By this time a young woman and her child had come into the department; they had gone straight up to the assistant, so the young man must have thought it was his golden opportunity. He took two jackets on their hangers off the rail, and one he dropped straight on to his open holdall, which he had placed on the floor immediately below the rail. He looked at the one jacket he still held, turned it round, and then replaced it on the rail. He then bent down as if to pick up his holdall and in doing so stuffed the jacket inside and quickly zipped the bag up. Then he picked it up and walked very near to us to look at socks, or us. Of course I had not seen the actual happenings, but Mrs Brown described everything to me a little later.

The man was now standing by the side of us, so Mrs Brown said to me, "I think we'd better have this one," picking up a blue shirt in a box. Then she said, "Where are the ties? We can't give a shirt without a tie." Well, you see, we had to let the young man think we were just plain shoppers.

We moved away to the tie stand, and this time Mrs Brown had her back to the young man and I kept him under observation while apparently still looking at ties. This time the young man had his holdall on the floor and a pair of socks in his hand. The very next instant his hand went into his pocket, still holding the socks. He then took his hand out of his pocket and no socks. Now doubts set in: had I seen socks in his hand in the first place? Perhaps not – but, yes, I *had* seen a pair of blue plaid socks in the hand that had gone into his pocket. Here we go again: he was holding another pair, a green plaid pair, in his right hand. Yes, yes, it was going towards his right jacket pocket – yes, straight in, and out came an empty hand.

'Crumbs, I feel ill. Now, don't panic – Mrs Brown is with me.'

At that moment I didn't know Mrs Brown had seen the jacket episode; I thought all he had taken was the socks.

When he moved away I mouthed to Mrs Brown, "He's got socks in his pocket."

She nodded.

We selected a tie and together we went to the counter. The young man looked about him, picked up his holdall and wandered over to the display of trousers. As he put the holdall on the floor under the rail of trousers he unzipped it. I still kept him under observation. Mrs Brown made our 'purchase' and the assistant knew something was up. He took a long time over wrapping the goods, but the young man still stood looking at trousers.

Now, we couldn't leave the department before him, or even leave the assistant, without it looking suspicious; so Mrs Brown whispered to the assistant, "Go and get some change and take a long time."

In a fairly loud voice he said, "I'm so sorry, madam – I have no change. Could you wait a minute while I get some?"

Mrs Brown said, "Yes, all right."

As the assistant left the department I saw the young man drop a pair of trousers on to the top of his holdall, and with his foot he shoved them into the bag. He continued looking through the display, and then, when the assistant returned, the young man bent down, zipped up the bag, picked it up and walked slowly from the department.

Mrs Brown turned to me, winked and said, "I think that's all we need here today, Lucy. Shall we go?"

We followed the young man. He left by the front door. We were very soon right behind him. Coo, he was tall and big! Mrs Brown is about 5 feet and I'm only about 4 inches taller. If he'd wanted to run, we couldn't have caught him; so we crossed the road and walked parallel to him away from the shop. Several times he looked behind him. We were hoping to see a policeman, or at least a man we knew, but no – no one. What we were to do?

We had just about summoned up enough courage, energy, adrenalin and willpower, to take the plunge to stop him, when he turned into a large building. We followed and as we entered a man came out. We stopped this man and asked him if he'd seen a young man enter the building.

"Well," he said, "if you mean Paul, he just passed me."

Mrs Brown said, "What's this place?"

I was able to tell her it was the back entrance to a college.

The man said, "Can I help you?"

Mrs Brown said, "Well, we're store detectives and we'd like to have a word with the young man you called Paul."

The man said, "I'll get him."

In a few minutes he returned with Paul. Yes, it was the young man we'd seen in the shop, but there was no sign of the bag.

Mrs Brown said, "I must ask you to come with us back to the store."

Paul said, "Oh yes, I'll come. I'm afraid I did take some things."

We were so amazed that we forgot about the holdall. We all returned to the shop, and in the manager's office we told the manager what had happened. He decided to call the police. With this, Paul burst into tears.

Have you ever witnessed a big, burly, twenty-two-year-old, blonde, blue-eyed, gorgeous hunk of man crying? Mrs Brown and I felt awful. He was a student and would be thrown out; he had let his mother down; she had struggled since his father had left them for another woman – all this between the sobs, great heaving sobs, and great blows in a large red handkerchief.

Right, that was it – I decided that no more would I do this rotten job, breaking mothers' hearts, ruining boys' chances. If we hadn't seen him, no one else would have done and he wouldn't be in the trouble he was in. If only I'd minded my own business! All this was going through my mind while we were waiting for the police to come.

A tap came on the door and two big, burly police officers entered.

"Bloody hell!" was uttered by one of them. "Not you again!"

He grinned and said, "Well, it is six months since I was caught. I've had a good run."

I was glad my letter of resignation was only in my mind. What a softie I was! No more would I be taken in. Perhaps that early experience has stood me in good stead. Never since have I allowed my own feelings to enter into any case.

Anyway, after the initial shock of realizing he really was a crook, Mrs Brown and I together remembered about the holdall. We told the police and one of them went to collect the bag from Paul's room. The other police officer took Paul to the police station, where he was duly charged with stealing one jacket, two pairs of socks, one pair of trousers and the holdall. Apparently he had stolen the holdall from the luggage department of the store before we saw him in the menswear department. Three weeks later he was charged at the magistrates' court and fined £25. We got our goods back.

Twice afterwards I saw Paul in town. He had not been thrown out of college, so his mother's heart wasn't broken; and each time I saw him he stopped and we chatted like old friends. It's a strange world.

Mrs Brown returned to Head Office and I continued walking the floorboards of the store.

It was getting near to Christmas when an assistant in the menswear department (in fact, it was the gentleman who had been discussing his plants when we started to watch Paul) came to me and said, "I wonder if we'll lose one or two sheepskins this winter."

I said, "Pardon?"

He said, "Every winter we have an old boy come in and walk out with a sheepskin coat on his arm. Stuart, our junior, saw him last year, and, not knowing what else to do, went up to the old boy and just took it from him as he walked down the road with it on his arm. About four days later another sheepskin had gone. We never knew if it was the old boy or not."

Funnily enough, about a week after this conversation Stuart came up to me in the cosmetics department and said, "The old boy is in the menswear department."

Right – I was ready for him. I casually walked into the menswear department and there was this old boy. He had a ring of white hair round the back of his head; otherwise he was bald. I suppose he was about sixty to sixty-five years old. He wore a short brown jacket and light summer trousers – certainly not suitable for winter weather. He had on sandals and no socks. I felt sorry for him. He was thin.

'Now, come off it!' I said to myself. Surely I'd learnt from my experience with Paul! This old boy had had a warning when Stuart stopped him the year before, so I doubted if he would take anything this year, but here he was, looking at sheepskin coats costing about £70. Good God, he was taking one off the rail and off its hanger! He carefully folded it over his arm and was leaving the department.

Perhaps we'd tempted him a bit: only I and one other customer were in the department and all the assistants had found some reason to disappear.

Mr A slowly walked out with me behind him, and the coat was on his arm. I was shaking like a leaf in a whirlwind. I was so sure he'd clobber me when I went to stop him. I looked round for a male assistant, but they'd all hidden themselves very well. There was not one in sight. Oh well, I was paid a shilling more per hour than the assistants; if I was going to get 'done', that was part of my job.

I followed Mr A outside the shop, and as he went to walk away I went up to him and said, "I'm a store detective and you've not paid for that." I pointed to the coat on his arm.

Suddenly I was surrounded by four male assistants from the shop. They had come to protect me, shilling or no shilling – bless them all! We all went back to the manager's office, where I told the manager what had happened.

The manager said to Mr A, "Are you the man who took a sheepskin coat last year and the year before, and the year before?"

"Yes," said Mr A. "You see, if I'm caught, I get free bed and board at the police station for a week, and sometimes the magistrates' court sends me to prison for six months. If I'm not caught, I sell the coat and then have some money."

What was the answer to this?

The manager told Mr A, "You'd better leave. I have the coat back and there seems little point in calling the police."

Mr A said, "Well, where can I go? It's now snowing, and if you don't call the police I shall put a brick through your front window. You'll have to call them then. And think of the mess – broken glass. It'll cost you to replace the glass. The police phone number is XYZ 111 – go on, call them. I really do want to go inside for the rest of the winter."

The manager was so shocked. We'd never before had a shoplifter begging for the police to be called. Whatever should we do? The manager decided to phone the chief security officer and ask his opinion. He rang, but he was out, so it was up to us to decide. OK, rather than have broken windows we called the police and explained it all.

Incidentally, while all this was going on, the manager had got his secretary to go to our canteen and get a meal for Mr A – steak-and-kidney pie, peas and potatoes, jam roly-poly and custard – and he was tucking into it while we were chasing ourselves silly, wondering what to do with him. He finished his meal as the police arrived.

"Hello," said a police officer. "We thought we'd see you again soon."

Off they merrily went to the police station.

The manager and I went to the canteen to get our lunch, but we found we were too late. It was closed. I began to wonder which side of the law I would do better to be on.

Mr A spent one week in custody at the police station, and after appearing at the magistrates' court got a sentence of four months in prison. This, he said as he left the dock, was just about right and would see him through the rest of the cold days.

A year gradually passed by and one cold December afternoon, a year almost to the day since I had stopped him, I saw him walking away from our menswear department with a sheepskin coat on his arm.

I followed him outside and said, "You've not done it again, have you?"

He replied, "Yes, love. How are you?"

I said, "Give me the coat and off you go. I can't charge you with shoplifting because I didn't see you take it."

The poor old boy's face fell. He probably remembered his meal at the shop, and knew he wouldn't get one again this year. He handed me the coat and wandered off up the road. He turned and waved to me.

He shouted, "Don't worry, love – I'll be OK."

I returned with the coat.

What a job! I felt mean if I caught anybody; and oh, how mean I felt *not* catching Mr A! I tried to get myself interested for the rest of the day, but it was just not possible. I decided to find Mr A if I could and give him a couple of quid.

I then received a telephone call from a colleague in a food store in town. She said, "A man who I just caught pinching a bottle of gin, and who has just been taken to the police station, begged me to ring you. He referred to you as that sweet girl who is the store detective at the department store. He asked me to tell you that he was now OK."

I burst out laughing and my colleague said, "Whatever's going on? Do you know him?"

I said, "Let's meet for a coffee."

We did and I explained.

We both heard later that the welfare worker had traced Mr A's sister, who lived in Manchester, and he was found a room to live in near her. Whether this worked out or not I don't know. Although every December I looked out for him, I never saw him again and we never again lost another sheepskin coat. It could be that the reason we never lost another coat was because instructions were received from Head Office that all expensive coats had to be kept locked up; or maybe Mr A was happy and stayed in Manchester.

Now for one that got away. In town (not London, ours) all the fairly large shops that had stands with sunglasses on display were congratulating themselves on the wonderful way nearly all their sunglasses had been sold. Well, they all thought they had been sold. In actual fact, a gang of youths, as we later found out, had been pinching them. Anyway, back to the start: as I said, the shopkeepers were congratulating themselves and ordering more sunglasses. It was only the beginning of June, and although we seldom see the sun in this country of ours we steadfastly maintain that summer extends at least through June, July and August, so more sunglasses were ordered and duly arrived.

In the meantime my colleague, Betty, had caught a young man in her store with two pairs of sunglasses in his pocket. She had seen him take a pair from the display and put them into his pocket. He then left the store. She caught him as he crossed the road, and he admitted taking two pairs. While talking to him, she discovered it was the in thing to knock off a new pair every day. Some of the lads had as many as twenty pairs each.

Betty told all the other detectives in town, including me, so when our new delivery arrived and the sunglasses were placed on display I kept watch. It was a Thursday and it was really quite quiet. A few old-age pensioners wandered around the store. Lunchtime brought in the usual workers from offices and shops around us, for their usual meander through during their lunch hour; then the afternoon came and gradually passed until the bell went and it was time to go home. No one had been interested in the sunglasses at all. In fact, all day only two people had hesitated by the stand and then only looked and did not touch. Mind you, it had been pouring with rain all day.

Friday dawned. I travelled to the shop on my usual bus, sitting by the fellow-traveller I always sat by.

"Yes, the weather was dreadful yesterday. Yes, it does seem brighter today. Here we are. All off."

I crossed the road, entered the shop and went straight to the department where the sunglasses were. I was there to stay.

At eleven thirty precisely four youths entered the shop. I could see the front doors from where I was standing. I must admit I was very bored and was wondering what to get my family for dinner that evening. The kids had said they were fed up with salad, so I was wondering. Suddenly I noticed the youths looking around them.

My insides said, 'Here we go again.'

The tallest of the gang sauntered up to – yes, the sunglasses. He took a metal-rimmed pair from the display and put them on. He looked all around him with them on. A second lad, wearing a green open-necked shirt, came up to him and said something. The first lad turned back to the stand and looked into the mirror provided for customers to see if they like the look of themselves in the glasses they've chosen. The third and fourth youths joined the other two and they were all very raucously taking glasses off the stand, trying them on and exchanging them with one another.

Realizing I couldn't cope with four shoplifters at once, I was frantically trying to attract the attention of any male staff member who happened to be in the vicinity. At the same time I was trying to watch the four youths. After, I suppose, a couple of very long minutes the shop's accountant (a nice young man) came past.

I grabbed his sleeve and said in a quiet voice, "I've got trouble. Four youths are pinching sunglasses. I need help. Get outside the door and wait to help me. He pushed off and I stood examining make-up – or so the youths thought. I saw the tall boy take the glasses off his face, fold them up and put them straight into his pocket. He then picked up another pair, this time with white rims. He pulled off the label and threw it on the floor. He put the glasses on and wandered away from the display. I was stuck. Did I follow that youth or stay and watch the other three? I looked at the three, and then looked back to where I had last seen the tall youth standing. He had gone – completely vanished. Well, at least I knew whom to watch now. I saw the boy in the green shirt pick up a fancy orange-and-red pair of glasses. He didn't even look round. He put them straight into his pocket. The third youth, whom I had noticed wearing glasses when he came in, now had a pair of clip-on sunglasses on his own. Fortunately for me, he hadn't removed the price ticket, which was stuck on to the wire piece that goes across the nose. I say 'fortunately' because without it I wouldn't have known they weren't his. I hadn't seen him pick them up. The fourth lad had his hands in his trouser pocket.

The three lads walked through the departments, gradually getting nearer the exit door. I slowly followed them through the door and caught up with them. The accountant was standing across the road with a male assistant. I nodded and they walked across the road towards me. The three youths had started to walk down the road. We followed. Then I tapped the green-shirted boy on the shoulder. He spun round and I said, "I'm a security officer." He looked as if he was going to make a run for it, so I grabbed his arm. The youth who was wearing glasses ran straight out into the road and straight into the side of a passing car. He rebounded into the arms of the accountant. The male assistant grabbed the third youth.

With struggles we got all three back to the office in the shop, where we recovered seven pairs of sunglasses from those three youths. They were all sixth-form boys from a local grammar school. We never did find out who the fourth boy was. The youths we caught were all taken to the police station and charged with stealing, but they all said there were only three of them in the shop that day, so I had to accept that one got away.

The police did visit the local schools and they informed all pupils that if any more were caught stealing, the penalties would be very severe.

At the end of August, about three months after I caught the boys and after a dreadfully dull, wet summer, nearly all the extra sunglasses bought because the shop managers thought they had had a good sale in sunglasses were still unsold (but unstolen as well) on their display stands.

THE POLICE AND US

As store detectives our powers of arrest were very different from those of the police. If we suspected a person, we could only suspect; but police officers could ask them to open their bags and explain themselves without any recriminations. So we sometimes called the police to help us. We had to be very certain of our facts before they liked helping us, but there were times when only they could deal with a situation. By the time I'd been with my firm for about three years I'd got to know our local police officers quite well and could go straight to anyone at the police station without being 'told off', as on my first visit, whenever I really needed their help.

It was a cold winter Thursday afternoon. It was pay day for us – not that that enters the tale, but the fact that it was pay day tells me it must have been a Thursday. At about three forty-five I noticed a young lady enter the shop. She was carrying a shopping bag, which appeared empty. She was also carrying a brown handbag. She seemed very, very uneasy. She kept looking about her. Perhaps she was looking for her boyfriend. She stood by the jewellery counter looking at chain necklaces. Why on earth was her right hand screwed up? And why was she poking at the necklaces in such a strange way? I wondered and watched.

Suddenly a voice behind me said, "Hi!" It was my friend Julia. "Have you time for a coffee?"

I turned and said, "I don't think so."

Not everyone I know knew what I did, but my closest friends did. Julia had been one of my bridesmaids and we were and still are, I hope, good friends; so she often called into my shop when she was in town doing her shopping to see if I was free for a quick cuppa. I looked back towards the jewellery counter and the young lady had gone. Had she stolen anything or not?

I turned to Julia and asked her to walk through the shop with me. She agreed, and in the underwear department we saw the young lady again. Earlier her shopping bag had seemed empty, but now it was bulging.

I couldn't see into it, so I quickly said to my friend, "Push off."

So off she went, and I followed the young lady into the dress department. She stopped by the rail of day dresses – beautiful, expensive dresses. She looked around her and selected a pink polyester dress in a size 10. She was a tiny person. She went up to an assistant and asked if she could try the dress on.

The assistant grinned and said, "Of course, madam." She threw back the curtains of the fitting room and ushered the young lady inside.

A few other customers wandered about. I continued to look at dresses, keeping my eye on the fitting room with the young lady in it.

The assistant was talking to another customer when the young lady peeped through the curtains of the fitting room. What she saw must have pleased her, because out she came, looking about her. She did not return the pink dress to the rail, but selected another pink dress – perhaps I should call it a rose-coloured dress as it was a deeper shade of pink than the first one – and a pale-blue patterned dress. Back into the fitting room she went without speaking to the assistant or letting her know she now had three dresses in the fitting room. I watched and waited. A few more customers entered the department, and eventually out of the fitting room came the young lady.

She handed the first pink dress to the assistant and said, "I'm sorry – pink isn't my colour."

The assistant replied, "Have you tried any more?"

The young lady said, "No, I haven't time," and off she went.

I went to enter the fitting room she had come out of to check that the other two dresses weren't still in there, but I was a little too late; another customer had got in there first, so again she slipped away. I had no proof she was shoplifting, though I felt she probably was.

I followed her down the stairs and out of the front door.

I was hoping to meet a police officer. She walked along the main street and into the post office. After pausing for a few seconds I went into the post office, but I could not see her anywhere. I carefully looked around, but she wasn't there. She had not passed me and there was no other exit. Strange! Again I looked around, and then I saw the photo booth in the corner. The curtains were drawn, but I could see a woman's legs inside. Have you seen those photo booths? A curtain comes only three-quarters of the way down the opening. Of course, I could tell they were a woman's legs, but were they hers? I knew she was wearing a blue overcoat and carrying a brown shopping bag and brown handbag, but were those legs hers? They had on a pair of brown fur boots, which matched the gloves and handbag I had seen. But wait! The legs were the wrong way round – the feet were pointing towards the back of the booth. She was obviously not having her photo taken; she was facing the seat. No wonder I could not see her bags on the floor; they were on that seat. Now I was a bit more sure it was the young lady, so I just stood and watched the legs and feet. They shuffled a bit, and then she bent over a little and I saw the hem of her coat. Yes, it was her. The coat was the blue one I'd been following. I peeped this way and that, trying to get a peep inside that booth, but the curtain was across the gap as if it was nailed to the sides.

'Ah!' I thought. 'If I drop a coin, I could get down on my knees looking for it and possibly then look inside.' I got my purse out and took out a twopenny piece. I thought, 'If it rolls completely out of sight, I shan't go broke, whereas I would miss ten pence even though it's not long since I've been paid. I shall have to see about a rise – oh dear, yes.'

Carefully I dropped my coin on the floor, but just as I was following its progress towards the booth a woman shrieked at her son behind me, "John, pick up that lady's money for her," and dear little John rushed over and whipped up the coin from the floor, where it had settled right at the opening of the booth. Little John handed the money to me, and his shrieking mother rushed up to me and said in a loud voice, "I'm trying to bring my child up to care for others and look after older folks. This world of ours has no manners and it is up to the young mothers of today to see the next generation are polite to their elders – don't you agree?"

I was struck dumb. My lady from the photo booth had come out and walked away through the front doors of the post office while the torrent had issued from the young mother. Anyway, who was she calling older folks? Me? I didn't think I looked any older than she did. Never mind about that, I must follow my lady. Without as much as a thank you to young John, I rushed out.

I'm sure I heard John's mother shrieking to someone else, "Really! Some people! How am I expected to bring up children decently with people like her in this world?"

If the mother of John reads this, may I now say thank you to him for picking up my twopenny piece and messing my plans up.

Away down the road I ran. There she was entering Woolworth's. Breathlessly I reached Woolworth's. Perhaps I *was* getting older. There was still no policeman or policewoman in sight. In I went. There she was at the far end. I quickly walked through, but as I got nearer I realized that although the coat was blue the face and hair did not belong to the young lady I'd been following. I stopped in my tracks and looked around. Woolworth's had many exits, and three floors. I'd lost her. Disheartened, I went through the other two floors, but there was no sign of her anywhere. I went down the stairs and out of a back exit, which led to a quiet road. I went slowly along this road. It was cold and I'd lost my suspect. I was fed up.

I thought I'd call in at the Wimpy for a cup of coffee before returning to the shop. By now it was five o'clock. I entered the Wimpy, ordered a coffee and went and sat down in the rear of the shop to await my coffee. I got out my notebook to write details of everything that had happened as I had to send a daily report of my doings to my chief.

Suddenly the door of the Wimpy opened and in came my suspect with two other young ladies. They were laughing and seemed very happy. All three had large shopping bags. They ordered coffee and came and sat at the table at the side of me. Whatever was I to do? I took a sip of my coffee. It must have been very hot as later at home I realized my mouth was burnt. I was in such a quandary that I didn't know I had burnt my mouth. Cor – one of the young ladies took several items from her bag. They were all unwrapped, though shops in our town always put purchases in their own paper bags. These goods – six pairs of tights, a pretty blue negligee and a blue cardigan – were obviously new, but not in any bags. I was sure they had been shoplifted. More laughter came from the ladies. I was dying to hear what they said, but taped music was issuing very freely from a speaker. It would have been hard enough to hear what someone sitting at my own table was saying, let alone what was being said at the table next to mine. More items were taken from bags and handed round among the ladies.

Suddenly one of them looked at her watch and said something, and all three quickly drank their coffee and out they went. It was now dark, but the street lights gave enough light for me to be able to follow the ladies. I felt I was not quite so noticeable. We all hurried along the road in the direction of the bus station, and that was where we eventually ended up. I still had not seen a police officer or even a traffic warden (traffic wardens were known to help us out).

There was a phone box at the bus station; so when the women all went into the waiting room, I phoned the police and told them quickly what had happened.

"OK," said the Sergeant, "keep them under observation and we'll be with you in three minutes."

I left the phone and waited outside the waiting room. I could see all three chatting together in there. For ten minutes I stood there, then my suspect made preparations to leave the other two. She picked up her bag and came out of the door. She crossed the road and got on to a village bus. The driver got into his place and started the engine, and off they went. Where, oh where were the police? Two more minutes went by and I saw two policewomen coming, almost at a running pace. Now I say *almost* at a running pace because I think police officers, like nurses, are not allowed to run. Anyway, they'd arrived. Later they explained why they were a long time coming. I pointed out the two ladies in the waiting room and explained that my suspect had got on a village bus and had gone. With that, a police car came into view. I was told by the policewomen to tell the sergeant driving the car about the one that got away. This I did. He asked which village the bus had gone to. I remembered and told him.

"Quick," he said, "Hop in."

I did and off we set. The traffic was bad. We seemed to be crawling very, very slowly. The Sergeant was getting quite cross at some stupid motorists blocking his progress. Eventually we got clear of town and traffic chaos and flew up the country roads towards the destination of the bus. As we swung round a corner there in front of us was the bus. We both sighed sighs of relief. The Sergeant lit himself a cigarette – he did offer me one, but as I don't smoke I helped myself to my vice, a Polo mint. We continued to follow the bus, and about two miles further on we reached the first stop of the village. The bus drew to a halt, and out poured half the travellers, but the lady still sat in her seat. We followed the bus to the next stop, and this time she got off the bus with several other travellers. I pointed her out to the Sergeant, who got out of the car and went up to her. On our journey I had explained to him that I thought she had stolen one chain necklace, some underwear and two dresses, one blue and one rose-pink.

I don't know what he said to her, but he brought her back to the car with her bags. She looked ghastly, absolutely shaken. I mean, fancy almost getting home with ill-gotten gains and relaxing on the way only to be met by a police officer when you get off the bus! The Sergeant and the lady, whom I shall now call Ann, got into the back of the police car, and the Sergeant took all the items out of Ann's bag. Yes – one necklace, two bras in boxes, a lovely orange slip, the blue negligee I had seen change hands at the café, several items for children, a pair of jeans, a jumper, a pair of pyjamas and, last of all, one rose-pink dress – the one I had seen go into the fitting room, but not come out. There was no sign of the blue dress.

The Sergeant asked me if I could definitely identify any of the items, and I said I could.

He then turned to Ann and said, "What have you to say?"

She said, "My sister gave them to me on the bus. She bought them for me during the week."

The Sergeant said, "Well, Mrs Smith, you must be psychic,

knowing this lady had the exact necklace and dress on her that you described to me on the way here." He then turned to Ann and said, "I'm now going to caution you that anything you say will be taken down in writing and may be given in evidence. We must now return to the police station."

Ann said, "But what about my kids?"

The Sergeant then found out that she had three young children. The oldest was nine and the youngest was five, so he could not leave them alone. He therefore radioed to headquarters for a policewoman to be sent out to Ann's address, and we then went to her home. Her husband was away. We went inside with Ann and waited. She gave the kids spaghetti on toast, and she gave the Sergeant and me a cup of tea each. Eventually the policewoman arrived and took over the household with instructions from Ann on how to get the kids to bed and whose turn it was for a bath, so we were able to leave – that is, the Sergeant, Ann and I.

About twenty minutes later we arrived at the police station. The Sergeant took Ann off to be charged and I went to make my statement.

While I'd been gadding about in the police car with a most handsome sergeant, the two policewomen I had left at the bus station had approached the other two ladies. Of course they both indignantly said how dare anyone suggest they had stolen anything. No, the policewomen could not look in their bags or they would sue the police for defamation of character. No, the two ladies would not go to the police station. In fact, there was quite a rumpus. Eventually one of the policewomen radioed in for help, and within three minutes four policemen arrived and forcefully took the two women to the police station. They continued to insist that they had not stolen any of the items found in their bags. There really was a haul: tights, make-up, underwear and, yes, the blue dress I'd seen go into the fitting room with Ann and apparently not come out.

When confronted with the fact that a store detective had seen the blue dress disappear, one of the women said, "How clever the store detectives are around here! They see things disappear. Well, if it disappeared, what's it doing here? Has it been reincarnated?" Then they did shut up.

I finished my statement and went home to a very worried husband. The time was now eight o'clock and I usually got in at about six.

The police officers took so long in getting to me, they explained, because there had been an accident outside the entrance to the police station and they couldn't get the car out. Anyway, they had come in the nick of time.

After explaining where I'd been, I got our supper, washed up and got the children to bed; then I fell into my own bed, exhausted. Next day I returned to the police station as I had been told to.

The Sergeant met me and told me the three women had been allowed home at eleven o'clock, after all three had admitted they had been shoplifting in town. The Sergeant then asked me into an interview room. After he unlocked the door I went in and was confronted with what looked to me like a shop full of items. The walls were covered with hangers holding dresses, skirts, coats, trousers and ladies' suits, and three large tables were piled high with jumpers, children's clothes, sheets, towels, children's shoes and eight pairs of ladies' shoes. In a large box on the floor were twenty-four assorted swimsuits and bikinis. In another, smaller, box, was make-up, including eyeshadow, eyebrow pencils, lipsticks, foundations, talc, perfume and deodorants. I was struck dumb, and it took me the next six hours to sort out what goods in that room had come from our shop, list them and make another statement out for the police stating what I had identified. The value of goods stolen from our shop came to £215 17s. 6d. The police officer then informed me that the three ladies said they had been taking goods for the past eighteen months. When the police visited their homes, the ladies had given up all the items they had stolen.

I returned to the shop and went straight to the manager and explained what I'd been up to. Well, I had been missing from the shop since four fifteen the previous day. It was now three thirty. Later I got a letter of congratulation from my chief at Head Office. Also I got a rise in salary. That might have been because I'd had a good catch, or it might have been because I'd been with the firm four years and increases usually came every two years (I'd had one increase two years previously).

Six weeks later the three ladies appeared in court. Two had

previous convictions and were fined £70 each. The third lady, Ann, had no previous convictions and the magistrates said she'd been led astray by the other two; she was put on probation for two years. As some of the stolen goods had been used, we were granted restitution and Ann had to pay £20, the other two ladies had to pay £25 each.

Another time I needed the help of the police was towards the end of my working days with the store. One Saturday (yes, I worked every Saturday) I was in the menswear department. It was a warm sunny day. A young smartly dressed man with fair hair was looking at suits. He had apparently nowhere to put anything if he was a shoplifter, so my gaze wandered around the department. A husband and wife were arguing over the colour of a tie, a child was running through the department pursued by a puffing father, and a couple were looking at shirts. The couple had a large shopping bag with them. I moved closer to them. The bag was full of shopping: groceries, including a loaf of sliced bread perched precariously on top. There was no room for stolen goods there.

I was about to wander off when I casually glanced at the young man. He had undone his jacket and there appeared to be a bulge under his right arm. Everything seemed to go quiet. The young man was walking towards me. Yes, there was a definite bulge under his jacket. Should I stick my foot out, and if he fell over it he might drop whatever was under his jacket? But it might just have been the way his jacket hung, now that it was undone. In any case, by this time he'd passed me and he was on his way out. I followed on wooden legs. I never did get used to seeing something pinched.

Out he went, and so did I, across the road, down a narrow side street. He was holding his right arm in a funny position. As he crossed the road he did appear to look back, but each time fortunately I was hidden from his view by other people. Round a bend he went. I followed – not too quickly. As I rounded the corner I saw him disappearing into the entrance of the multistorey car park. I hurried on and saw the lift he had got into stop at deck 4. I went up the steps at a gallop – I hate lifts, but my heart and lungs don't like stairs, so as I reached deck 4 I was gasping for breath. But I had to find the young man with fair hair and see what was happening.

I looked around and I saw him just getting into a lovely maroon-coloured car with that year's registration letter on it. He sat in the driver's seat and had his back turned to the window. I could not see what he was doing, but I daren't get too close. Professional shoplifters have been known to get a bit nasty, and I didn't fancy leaping from car to car in my desire to get away from him driving at me (sometimes I felt like Policewoman). Back to reality: I just kept my distance and watched. He got out of his car, took off his jacket and pulled from his car a sort of raincoat, loose and baggy. Why on earth would he do that? It wasn't cold – in fact, it really was too warm for even a jacket.

He shut up the car and walked towards the lift. I didn't dare follow him in case he realized I'd been following him since he left the store. In any case, I wanted to have a peep in his car. I watched from the window on the stairway and saw him leave the building and walk back towards the shopping centre.

I went back to his car. I tried the handle, but of course it was locked. I must say I felt very, very guilty and if I'd been able to open a door I don't think I would have touched anything anyway. I couldn't, so that problem didn't arise. I peered through the window and saw his jacket lying on the back seat, obviously over something. There were a lot of papers and files on the front passenger seat, but I could see nothing incriminating.

I decided to get back to my shop. I had no proof about anything, so I returned. I went straight to the menswear department.

I was greeted by a very irate assistant: "Where the hell have you been?" he said. "I think a bloke in a dark raincoat just pinched a suit. Look – here's the hanger."

And there, true enough, was the empty hanger gently swinging.

The assistant went on: "I saw this bloke with the raincoat on. He had fair hair. He was looking at the suits and I thought to myself, 'Funny – a raincoat today!' I went up to him and he said he was only looking, so I left him and served a lady with a shirt. A nice green-striped one, it was, and when I turned the man had gone and I saw the hanger; so I wanted you and no one knew where you were. Anyway, you're here now – can't you go and find him?"

I said, "Let's phone the police."

This I did. I explained to a sergeant all that I'd seen happen. I told him where the car was, gave him the registration number and rang off.

About three hours later I received a call from the police station. Would I go and identify some goods? So off I went to the police station. This, by the way, had moved premises during my years with the store. It was now situated about a mile from us across town. It was a purpose-built place, with everything clearly labelled, and everyone had to wait for electrically locked doors to open when a police officer said so. There was no more wandering about. Anyway, I was well known by this time and had no difficulty getting to the right department, CID.

I was shown into an interview room and there was quite a pile of stuff, including our menswear-department suit, a large holdall with one of our price tickets on it, a travelling clock with our label, and quite a lot of other items not belonging to our firm.

Apparently after I phoned the police two plain-clothes police officers went and found the man's car. They parked their old Anglia just behind his car and waited. He returned to his car, threw the holdall into the boot, took off his coat and put that inside the car, put his jacket on, lit a cigarette and got into the car. With that, the police officers got out of their car, went up to him and tapped on his window.

He opened it and one of the police officers said, "We're police officers and believe you are in possession of stolen property."

He, of course, denied it, but they all went back to the police station. The total value of stolen goods found in the man's car came to £130, and he later admitted to stealing all the items. He was a salesman and covered quite a large area. No one can be sure that he pinched in every town he visited, but I will say he knew what he was doing. From his statement I learnt that on his first visit to our shop he succeeded in pinching the trousers from the suit (that was what the bulge was in his jacket); the second time, when he had the raincoat on, he pinched the jacket. He was kept at the police station and appeared before the magistrates the following Monday. He pleaded guilty and was fined £50.

WOMEN SHOPLIFTERS AND AN HONEST VIP

As I told you, the first person I ever caught shoplifting was a woman who took a table lamp. I think that was the largest item I ever saw being concealed and taken. Then there was the case of Mrs B.

About eight months after starting my new life as a store detective I had got into quite a happy rut. My day started by getting my husband off to work, then my two sons off to school. I had found out by now that there was no sense in having an au pair because the two I had had in the eight months had been a disaster. Twice I'd been called to school because my youngest son, then aged five years, had not been collected. I got a taxi both times and collected him. On the first occasion the au pair had washed her hair and didn't want to go out with wet hair; on the second occasion she had simply gone to sleep (she had been to a very late party the night before and was tired). I was very cross with her and she left two weeks later.

The second au pair was a nice girl and very good at collecting my son from school, but she didn't like getting up in the morning, so I often went to work and left her in bed. When I returned she had seldom done even her own washing-up. She seemed to use every saucepan I had for her dinner, and before I could get our evening meal I had to wash up her saucepans.

After she decided to return to Spain, her home, I talked things over with my husband and my shop manager and it was decided I could work from nine thirty until three thirty, and my mother-in-law would help out at holiday times. My own mother lived 175 miles away, so I could not call on her for help. We thought we'd try without live-in help.

As I said, I had got into a nice rut. After getting the boys ready for school, I took the youngest on my bike, and his brother, aged seven, went on his own bike. I dropped them off at about eight forty. I rushed home, took the dog for a five-minute run up the road and back, fed him, fed the budgies and made the beds (I can leave the washing-up, but I can't go out leaving unmade beds; they were only pulled up but they looked tidy). I then made a cup of coffee, put on my working clothes (best), washed up if there was time, found my handbag, made sure the windows and doors were shut and that the dog had water, and put the key in a special place because I now employed a local woman to come in and clean three times a week and she needed to get in. Now I was off – a quick run to the corner of the road and on to the bus at nine twenty, arriving at the shop at nine thirty.

I would wander around the shop until ten forty; then I would go to our smashing canteen for a lovely cup of coffee and a ham roll. How I enjoyed that elevenses every day!

Well, now I can get back to Mrs B. I had just collected my coffee and roll when the canteen assistant informed me that I was wanted in the underwear department. She said she'd get me a fresh coffee when I returned and would keep the roll to one side. Off I went to the underwear department.

A young assistant flew up to me and, trying not to shake, said out of the corner of her mouth, "That woman" – nodding towards the back of a customer who was carrying a large yellow carrier bag – "just pinched a black bra."

I said, "Are you sure?"

The assistant said, "Yes."

At that moment the customer looked straight at us both, and I felt sure she must realize I was a store detective.

However, I thought I'd better try to act like a customer, so I said to the assistant, "My husband is fed up with me in nice undies. I want to look at some sexy ones."

The assistant, trying hard not to laugh, brought out a tray of daring undies as Mrs B walked past.

The assistant said, "But I'm afraid we don't go to your size, madam."

I agree I looked plump, but I did have a big coat on. The assistant by this time was beside herself with hidden laughter.

Mrs B walked out of sight, so I had to follow her. I left my laughing assistant friend and I followed Mrs B to the shoe department. Well, as in most stores, only one shoe of a pair is displayed on stands. This does help to prevent shoplifting – no one wants just one shoe. It also stops customers trying shoes on without the assistant's help. Most customers want to try on both shoes. The second shoes were kept in their boxes on wall stands all around the department. Mrs B went straight up to the boxes, took a shoe out, held it in her hand and proceeded to look along the display of single shoes. The department was quite busy, so she was not observed by any assistant. Eventually she found the 'mate' to the one she had in her hand and removed it from the display. As she walked away from the department she dropped both shoes into her yellow carrier bag. I was astonished at the cool way she did it, so I presumed the assistant in the underwear department was right about the bra.

Mrs B had by now made her way to the haberdashery department. She looked about her, and eventually went up to the rail of aprons. They were all hanging from hangers on a rail. My mind changed course for a moment: aprons meant kitchen; kitchen meant food – my roll and coffee. My stomach was rumbling. Come on, woman – get on with it. Pinch it, or get out. Whatever happened I wouldn't be free for at least an hour and a half. I would stop her for the shoes, then we'd go back to the manager to wait for the police. 'Come on, missus!' While I was thinking these thoughts she took from the hanger a yellow sort of patchwork apron, rolled it up and dropped it straight into her yellow carrier bag. An assistant was about to approach the woman.

I stepped in front and growled, "Go away."

She fled.

Off we went – Mrs B had picked up the carrier bag and walked away.

'Go on out,' I willed her; but no, my thoughts didn't get to her.

I followed her to the children's department. Here an assistant went straight up to her. Could she help the lady? Mrs B replied that she was only looking around. I felt like adding "and pinching", but of course I didn't. I just kept a respectful distance.

I've often wondered why shoplifters don't think to themselves, 'That woman has been in every department I've been in.' I suppose they just don't think they've been seen.

The assistant returned to chinwag with another assistant, perhaps thinking she'd done her best to prevent pilfering by asking if she could help the customer.

Mrs B picked up two girls' blouses from a display set out on a flat surface. She held them in her hand for a few minutes and then she turned her back to the two chatting assistants; and as she started to walk away from the department she dropped them into her yellow carrier bag.

You may be wondering how I could see all this happening. Well, I was in the next department peering through a rail of dresses. It had been beautifully placed, and I could see all Mrs B was doing without her seeing me. However, she had to come through the department I was in to go anywhere else. I didn't want to risk her seeing me, so I took a dress from the rail and slid into a fitting room. I peeped through the curtains and watched her walk past.

I thought I'd better give her a couple of seconds before I popped out and went after her, so I counted quite quickly to sixty. Then I slowly emerged. She'd gone – nowhere to be seen. I fairly ran to the top of the stairs, but there was no sign of her anywhere. I quickly went down the stairs and out into the street. Yes, there she was – halfway down the road on the other side.

I hurried down the road, caught up with her and said the usual party piece: "I am a store detective and you have left with a pair of shoes and two children's blouses."

She said, "Yes, and a bra and a pair of pants and two slips."

I said, "Well, we must return to the manager."

She said, "OK. You know, I wondered about you. I saw you in the underwear department, but thought you didn't look bright enough to be a detective. After all, I thought you'd hardly be asking someone about sexy underwear if you were clever enough to be a defective – I mean, detective."

Mrs B and I returned to the manager's office. I reported the facts, and I must admit I was rather sorry the police had to be called. Mrs B seemed such a nice person. She accepted she'd been caught and really had been no trouble to me. In fact, after her court case, at which she was fined £10, she often shopped in our store. If she saw me, she'd come up, take my arm and say, "Let's do my shopping together. Then you don't have to watch me. That really was the first time I'd ever been shoplifting. It seemed so easy, but now I know people do watch."

I told her that it was the assistant who had first seen her and sent for me.

She said that after the initial shock of being caught and treated as a criminal she realized it was good she was caught because she'd never do it again.

I patted myself on the back. I'd stopped someone getting themselves into serious trouble.

Two years later I read in the paper that Mrs B had been caught shoplifting in another store in town. When the police searched her home, it was stuffed full of new goods, dresses, shoes . . . oh, just about everything. Apparently after getting a fine of only £10 for the offence committed in our store she thought she'd learnt enough about store detectives to avoid being caught – and, indeed, if the fine was only £10 it was quite worth the risk.

While the police were searching her house two ladies turned up to buy dresses. They thought Mrs B sold odd sizes and rejects for firms; they had no idea the goods were stolen. They told the police Mrs B often took orders from people for a specific type of garment and would get it for them from the wholesalers in a week to ten days. Of course, what she did was to pinch them. I was glad that not one item had been stolen from our firm. This time Mrs B landed up with a six-month prison sentence. I never met her again.

Oh yes – I eventually had my ham roll and coffee that first day at lunchtime.

Another incident involving a woman, or rather *women* shoplifters, happened two days before Christmas in my second year. I'd completed my own Christmas shopping – there was just some aftershave to get for Ron, my husband, from one of our sons. I wandered into the cosmetics department. A charming customer stood there in a beautiful fur coat – a most elegant woman. She had a beautiful leather handbag with shoes and gloves to match. Her hair was black and silky and held in a loose bun. She was talking to four beautiful girls, all with large dark eyes, and all had long black hair. There was also a boy aged about twelve years. He had a funny multicoloured woollen hat on his head. They were all talking in a foreign language, so I walked on and bought my aftershave and wandered off.

I was walking through the menswear department when I again saw the fur-coated woman, this time alone. She was holding a leather holdall, and a ticket was attached with our store's name on it. Funny! I quickly went to the luggage department and questioned the staff. Yes, they'd noticed the lady in the fur coat. They'd had a discussion about what nationality she was. I interrupted their vague thoughts and discovered that she had not purchased a bag.

"But look – there's a space on that stand," one of the assistants said. "Something's gone from there. I dusted all round not long ago, and that space wasn't there then."

Right – off I went to find my fur-coated lady. Running past me was the little chap in the funny woollen hat. I discreetly followed and he led me to his mother. As he reached her, he handed her a bottle of perfume. She looked around her and placed it into the bag. They moved upstairs to the separates department. Here she met the four young ladies again. They stood and chatted, and I was almost stamping my feet with fury – I couldn't understand a word. They then all turned and, leaving the boy outside, the five females entered the ladies' room. I followed. The mother, as I later found out she was, entered a toilet with the bag. After a few moments she came out without the bag. One daughter went into the same toilet with a carrier bag obviously containing items; she pulled the chain and came out with the carrier bag empty – it was folded up. Another daughter went into the same toilet – rustle, rustle. Out she came, then the mother returned to the toilet and after about three minutes came out carrying the bag.

I left the cloakroom and then they followed me. I wandered around to the underwear department, and they seemed quite happy to follow me. The boy had disappeared. I was busy pretending to look at slips when I noticed the daughter with the carrier bag – she unfolded it and placed it on the floor under a rail of bedjackets, pretty and expensive ones. I saw her slip a pale-blue one with swansdown on it straight into the open carrier bag. An assistant standing nearby also saw it, but she saw me and turned away.

If she had said anything to the girl, she might have said, "It dropped and I was about to take it out," or even, "I was going to pay for it."

Although I had my suspicions at that time I had not seen them actually take anything. I wanted that bedjacket to stay in the bag so that I could stop them outside. I really had no need to worry. I then followed them into the gown department and, without giving possible shoplifters who might read this book a clue how they did it, I saw a blue chiffon evening dress valued at forty-nine guineas disappear and two day dresses just vanish. Together we all wandered back to the casual-wear department. This time two lovely kilts and two pure-wool jumpers did the vanishing trick. I was completely fascinated. Never before had I seen stuff just go. They all trooped down the stairs. The boy was again with us. We all headed straight for the doors and out into the street. It had just started to snow.

I grabbed the arm of the lady in the fur coat and said, "Do you speak English?"

"Yes," she said, "of course."

I said to all of them, "I'm a store detective and you've left with goods you've not paid for."

"Ah, yes," said the lady, "it is lovely snow."

I said, "No – come inside."

She said, "No – I like to see snow. Our country is hot."

I said, "Come," and fairly dragged the coat off her back to get her inside.

Two assistants had come out from the shop and helped me get them back into the manager's office, which at any time was small. Now, with the manager, me, two assistants, the woman, her four daughters and one son, we were packed like sardines. It was decided also to use the secretary's office, and here we took from the bag (which was pinched) make-up, tights, jewellery, perfume and two folded umbrellas. From the carrier bag came two kilts, two jumpers and one day dress. The blue chiffon dress was concealed in the lady's pocket. In all £95 worth of goods was recovered, The police were called, but all five insisted they were so excited at seeing snow falling that they had forgotten to pay for the goods.

The lady took £500 from her handbag and said, "See!"

They were due to fly home that very evening. The police said it was possible they had forgotten after seeing the snow for the first time in their lives, and also they had plenty of money to pay for the goods. I tried to explain that they didn't see the snow until after they had left the store, but we just got our goods back and off they went.

The manager agreed with me that they had intended to steal the items, but as it was Christmas and they were, after all, leaving our fair city . . .

"Hah!" I said. "I'd have a coat like that if I pinched."

"Ah," said my wise manager, "do you sleep well?"

I said, "Yes, of course."

"Well," he said, "I don't suppose she does."

I wonder.

One lady shoplifter I shall not forget is Mrs C. It was ten forty-five on a Thursday morning in November, and I was in the casual-wear department when I saw Mrs C. She had with her her child, a girl of about three years. She was standing by a display of hangers holding ladies' slacks. She took a red pair from a hanger and held them in her left hand. I moved to the side of her and was looking through the stock. She moved away from the rails with the slacks still in her hand. She picked up her basket and moved to a nearby chair. Here she put the slacks into her basket and covered them with a paper bag. She called to her child and left the department. I followed her through the coat department, down the stairs to the ground floor and out of the front doors. Just outside she put her child into a pushchair and pushed her shopping further into her basket. She looked about her and then started to walk down the road.

I went after her and said, "Excuse me." She stopped and I went on: "I am a store detective and you've not paid for the slacks."

"Oh dear – yes, you're right."

I asked her to return with me to the manager's office.

On the way she said, "I don't know why I did it. My marriage is on the rocks."

As usual we came to the manager's secretary's office door. In we went, Mrs C and her child first.

The secretary looked up and said, "Hallo, Mary. What a surprise! Did you—?" Then she stopped dead when she saw me. Apparently Mrs C was a friend of the secretary.

We were quickly ushered into the manager's office, where I explained what had happened and the police were called. They arrived and took Mrs C and her child to the police station.

The secretary said she was absolutely dumbfounded when she saw me behind Mrs C. She'd known her for years; they'd been great friends. Although her marriage was at the moment going through a sticky patch, Mrs C had two children, a boy and girl, aged about twelve and fourteen, and she had just got herself a nice job as a secretary when out of the blue along came child number three. Mrs C had always blamed her husband, and he had started going out a lot to avoid being with his wife, who kept blaming him; so the marriage was very shaky. Mrs C went to court about two months later, and we were all delighted to hear she got a conditional discharge, and her husband and she were now much happier. So perhaps I did some good.

In the six years I was with the firm I apprehended 302 shoplifters, and only forty-nine of those were male. The rest were female. I never did total up the full cost of the goods recovered from the shoplifters I apprehended.

After about two years I was able to tell the time of day and day of the week by the regular customers. There were three ladies who always met every Thursday at ten thirty in the cosmetics department. They always wore the same clothes – not as one another, but as the ones they'd worn the week before and the week before that. I never did find out who they were, but they used to wander round from department to department looking at fashion clothes – never trying any on, but just looking. Then at twelve forty-five they would go to the ladies' room, powder their noses and then leave the shop.

One quiet day, out of curiosity, I followed them. They went to a local tea shop and had lunch. I suppose it was a girls' morning out. Possibly they had been school friends and then married and still remained friends.

Then there was the funny round-faced man from the local mental hospital who every day walked slowly through the shop, a newspaper under his arm, his hands behind his back, graciously nodding at all the assistants who were not busy. I never saw him speak to anyone or buy anything, or, in fact, even look at goods on display.

One customer who as far as I know only ever came in once set everyone looking, and also set them on their very best behaviour. All the young assistants became dewy-eyed when word got around. He came in to purchase a man's umbrella. He walked through the shop to the menswear department, where we usually had quite a number, but this day we had none. There had been such a lot of rain that we had sold out, so he went to our competitor and got one. He even had his photograph in the local paper buying the thing. It made our manager mad. You see, the customer was none other than Prince Charles. Menswear was never without umbrellas after that time. He was a student at our local university.

SOME WHO NEARLY GOT AWAY

It had been almost five weeks since I last caught anyone shoplifting. The sun shone brightly outside the shop. I was feeling completely useless. Can you imagine, for six hours a day and five days a week, just wandering around a shop trying to look like a customer, yet constantly on the watch for odd happenings?

Occasionally a sales assistant would say, "Mrs Smith, someone's taken an item from my counter."

I'd be disgusted with myself – obviously I just wasn't in the right place at the right time.

One Thursday lunchtime everywhere was quiet. It was almost siesta time. Some of the assistants were perched on stools, almost asleep; others were off on their lunch break. There were only about six customers and me, and everywhere the atmosphere was relaxed. A man wandered into the menswear department. He had on only a suit (a nice light-grey suit), a pale-blue shirt and a dark-blue tie. Although I've said he had on only a suit, of course he had shoes on too. What I meant was that he had on no big overcoat to shove anything under if he wanted to pinch something; so I sort of ignored him, but I couldn't. Many good store detectives seem to have this something that means we can almost smell a shoplifter. I tried to reason with myself. He was a nice-looking man and he had nowhere to hide anything. Why, oh why didn't I trust him? Again I tried to walk away, but I just couldn't. I felt I had those cement shoes on that I had when I caught my first shoplifter.

The man looked around and unfortunately our eyes met. I pretended that I was looking around at items on display. Had he realized what I was? He just stood in the department looking about him.

I gave myself a good talking-to: 'You know, you really are getting too bad. You've not caught a shoplifter for five weeks, so you look at everyone almost willing them to pinch.'

'No I don't,' I replied. 'I just feel this man *might*.'

'Come on,' I said, 'let's go for dinner. He's seen you and he must know what you do. After all, it must be obvious. Come on out of here – left foot, right foot.'

My body started to move out of the department, very, very reluctantly. I slowly moved away.

As I got to the shoe department the head of the department called out, "Mrs Smith, your shoes have come back." Three weeks earlier I'd sent them for repair.

"Oh, right," I said. "I'll take them."

I sat on a chair while she went to get them. She returned and I stood up to go to the cash desk to pay. As I did, the man entered the department. We sort of collided, and I promptly sat down again – not only from the collision, but from shock. When I'd last seen him, only a few minutes previously, he had on only his suit; now he was carrying a suit in a cleaner's plastic cover – you know, the sort cleaners put on when you've had clothes cleaned. I was dumbfounded. He hadn't got it with him when first I saw him, and he'd not had time to get out of the shop and go to the cleaners and come back. Where had it come from? Was I dreaming? Was I sure it was the same man? All this must have raced through my mind in between his knocking into me and my sitting promptly back on the chair.

He was saying to me, "I'm so sorry. Did you get hurt?"

As I looked at him I knew it was the same man I'd seen before.

"No, no," I said. "I'm fine." I jabbered on about getting my shoes repaired – I'd found this was the best place, always so quick and reasonably priced. The man muttered something, and then with his cleaned (?) suit turned to an assistant and asked for shoes, size 8, in brown suede.

He sat down and carefully placed his suit over another chair, and I saw gracefully dangling from the sleeve of the suit in the cleaner's bag was one of our price tickets. Now I really couldn't get off the chair – cement shoes, and now cement knickers. I was stuck.

'Pull yourself together, girl,' I thought. 'Take a peppermint out of your handbag and then pay for your shoe repairs; and if by then the man's nearly ready to leave, OK. If not, pretend you want to buy a pair yourself. Right, here goes – peppermint in, stand up, walk to cash desk, collect repaired shoes, pay, hope against hope no assistant will yell out, "Caught anybody lately?" as they sometimes do, put repaired shoes in bag, look round.'

The man had decided not to have shoes. He collected his plastic-covered suit and started to leave the department. I followed him. Together we reached the door. He held it open for me. I walked through.

I said, "Thank you," and as he followed me out I turned to him. We were now outside the door. In my next breath I said, "I am a store detective and you've not paid for that suit."

His face, I'll never forget it. He turned without a word and we re-entered the shop. This time I held the door for him. He turned and looked at me. He was still clutching the suit and I ushered him into the manager's office.

He sat in a chair and his first words were, "I thought you were ordinary. You didn't look bright enough. You can't be."

I looked at the manager and I think we both thought of the chief security officer's words at my interview: "There's nothing noticeable about her."

Well, another shoplifter had been apprehended. My suspicions – or my nose – had been right, but I had nearly messed it up by trying to get away from my instincts. Fortunately, everything turned out well. The man was later fined £25 at the local magistrates' court.

Another one that nearly got away was a middle-aged lady, very well dressed and beautifully spoken. I first saw her talking to a beauty advisor on the beauty counter. They were discussing the pros and cons of a particular night moisturising cream. The lady asked the advisor if she could see a particular item from the shelf. The beauty advisor turned and, as she did so, the lady's arm reached over the counter and I was certain a bottle of something shot up her sleeve –

or did it? The beauty advisor turned back and the lady's arms were at her sides, though she was clutching her right glove rather oddly. As they were talking the lady cautiously opened her handbag, which was hanging from her left arm. She was all smiles, continuing to talk to the advisor, who couldn't see what was going on. The lady's hands and bag were below counter level. I then saw the lady's right hand and glove disappear into her handbag. She then sort of shook her arm, and after a couple of seconds she withdrew her hand, shut her handbag and continued talking. I was fascinated. I mean, fancy pinching something from right under the assistant's nose! The talk was apparently coming to an end without a sale.

The lady was most polite, and as I moved a little nearer I heard her say, "Well, I must think it over. I agree with you: my skin is a little greasy. I'll be in again next week." And off she wandered.

The beauty advisor looked across at me and mouthed, "Next week and next week."

I went over and said, "What do you mean?"

She said, "Oh, she comes in every week and never buys a thing. One day I'll make her."

"Well," I said, "maybe it'll be today."

I turned to where I'd last seen her, but she had gone. Panic! I looked all around, but she'd gone. I looked out in the street, and in every department, but it was no good – she'd hopped it.

I returned to the beauty advisor and said, "Call me when she comes in again." I explained what I'd seen happen and how I'd lost her.

"Oh," she said, "madam always goes to our hairdressing salon after her visit to me."

'Hurrah!' I thought.

Up I went, and there I found her. Of course, I had to wait for her to have her hair tinted, washed and set and for her to leave the store before I could stop her for taking the bottle of expensive perfume without paying for it. She was later fined £5 at the magistrates' court.

Here is another one that nearly got away – well, it was actually two teenage girls. One afternoon during the last week of school term I was as usual wandering around the store. It was quite busy. Mums seemed to be getting ready for the long school holiday, enjoying their last days of freedom. They were looking at clothes and having a coffee with friends before being penned in for the next six weeks, when the only outings might be to the swimming pool, the zoo or the cinema. I'm sure any mum reading this knows the feeling. I did when I was a mum. That sounds odd – I'm still a mum, but now I'm a working mum so have a slightly different outlook on life.

Oh dear – back to my book! I do wander. I was, as I said, in the shop. It was about three o'clock when I noticed two teenage girls picking items up and looking about then in the haberdashery department. They were whispering quietly. I decided to keep them under observation. The fair-haired girl picked up a thimble. Her fingers closed all around it and they moved away. The fair-haired girl was looking around her. They went to the display of darning wool. The dark-haired girl picked up a card of grey darning wool and then screwed it up into a ball. They both looked about them and then slowly the dark-haired girl put her hand and the grey darning wool into her pocket. They spoke together, giggled, looked around them and sauntered off towards the doors into the street. They kept looking around them and I followed. Eventually we got through the doors.

I grabbed the fair girl's arm and said, "I'm the store detective."

With that both girls started to run. I was hanging on to the arm of the fair-haired girl, and she and I tumbled into a heap on the ground. The dark-haired girl had gone. I was determined to hang on to the one I was struggling with.

There were two men standing nearby and I called out, "Please can you help me?"

Both men turned and looked the other way. At the time I was cross, but later, on reflection, I realized that neither man could have known who was in the right. I could have been attacking the poor girl. And so often if you go to help someone, it means court appearances. Had I been in the position of those two men I would probably have turned away too. Anyway, the fair-haired girl and I struggled for a bit and eventually I did what I think is called a half nelson on her arm – that is to say I got her arm behind her back and twisted very slightly. She yielded and we marched back to the manager's office, where a very startled secretary and manager looked at us as we walked in. After all, we must have looked quite dreadful after our rolling about on the ground outside the shop.

As I explained the circumstances to the manager I tried to pull my hair straight and shake my clothes out a little. I told the manager that there was another girl involved and eventually the fair-haired girl told us who her friend was. Both girls were thirteen years old. The manager decided that instead of the police being called I was to take the fair-haired girl home and, on the way, visit the home of the dark-haired girl and explain the circumstances to both sets of parents. The fair-haired girl had told us that it was a dare going round their school.

In those days I couldn't drive so the manager phoned the warehouse and got a porter to get the company car and take the girl and me to her home. When he arrived I had a second fright: the porter had only one hand and a stump. He held the driving wheel with his right hand and moved the gear stick with his stump. He had to reach over with his right hand to release the button and apply the handbrake. However, we did reach the dark-haired girl's house.

I went in and explained to the parents, and they were quite horrified and thanked me and our firm for treating this childish prank in such a sympathetic manner.

About three days later the manager received a letter containing the purchase price of the darning wool and thimble and apologies from the two girls.

One day in my first summer as a store detective I will not forget. Everywhere in the shop was quiet. It was a Tuesday. I was working as usual from nine thirty until three thirty, wandering around. Nothing apparently was going on.

At one twenty-five the manageress of the swimwear department caught my eye as I wandered through her department. She said, "I think I'm losing my grip."

I asked, "Why?"

She said, "Well, this morning I put out six new swimsuits, all black-and-white. Some had skirts; some were without. One had a white plastic ring holding bra to pants. All were size 34 or 36, but I can't find a single one of them."

I suggested she'd not put them out, and offered to check her stockroom with her. Together we looked and, although there were two black-and-white ones, the delivery note which had come with them said eight, so that still left them six short. We went back to the department and searched – not one. We checked again. None had been sold, and the manageress asked her staff if anyone had tried on black-and-white swimsuits. The assistant said no, but two ladies at about eleven o'clock had tried on the expensive lilac one and the sunshine-yellow one. They didn't buy them.

The assistant suddenly went quite white and said, "I never put them back. Good God!"

She rushed to the rails and frantically searched – no sign of lilac or sunshine yellow. The lilac swimsuit cost £15 and the sunshine-yellow one cost £12. Checking the delivery note we found that the six black-and-white swimsuits were valued at £68, so the total cost of the missing swimsuits was £95. The manager was going to be pleased!

I asked the assistant for a description of the two women.

"Well," she said, "they seemed nice."

"Yes," I said, "but what did they look like?"

She just was not able to remember, except that one of the women wore a big amethyst ring on her right hand. It was square and surrounded by diamonds. I was just wondering what to do when my buzzer went.

I haven't yet mentioned my buzzer. Well, it was similar to a doctor's bleeper, and if it buzzed I had to answer the nearest telephone. I would then be told by our telephone operator where I was wanted.

I answered the phone and was told, "The police want to speak to you. I'll put you through."

With that the lady detective constable at our local cop shop said, "Hi. Have you lost any good clothes today?"

I said, "Well, I've just discovered we've lost eight swimsuits."

"Right," said the lady detective constable, "please find out if anything else has gone and then come here."

I put the phone down and on questioning other departments I

found two suits, one navy and one brown, had gone missing, and so had six Goray skirts.

I made my rather disgruntled way to the police station. I'd been in the shop and about £275 of stuff had been stolen. Ugh!

In the CID office I was confronted with a roomful of clothes. I identified the clothes as being similar to those sold in our store, but as no one had actually seen them taken by a customer we could not definitely say they came from our store. There are about eleven other branches of our store, and the items could have come from any of them.

The police officer said, "We are holding two ladies and a man on suspicion of stealing all these items, but we cannot get any proof."

What happened was that, at about two o'clock, a cleaner from a local supermarket was clearing up the rubbish from the back of his shop, and in doing so he stopped for a fag. While he rested on his broom he looked up the road. It was a beautiful day. A man was sitting in a large car, and he noticed a woman come up to the car, take some items from a bag and put them into the back of the car. The man and woman exchanged words and off went the woman again. There was no reason for the cleaner to think anything was amiss, so he resumed sweeping up. He didn't fancy returning to sweep up inside, so he moved the dustbins around and decided to wash down the part of the yard where the dustbins stood. He got his bucket and long-handled scrubber, filled the bucket with water and disinfectant and proceeded to scrub. After he finished he decided to have another fag before going inside. His work had taken him about twenty-five minutes. As he was lighting up he noticed the car and man were still in the same place, and two women were taking clothes out of carrier bags and throwing them into the boot of the car. Somehow he didn't like the look of what was going on.

All staff have basic training in security and know that if something doesn't seem right they should inform their store detective or manager. On this day their store detective was away, and so the cleaner found the manager and told him what he'd seen happening. Together they went to the back of the shop and looked up the road – and yes, the car was still there.

The manager said, "Well, I'll go and have a look."

The cleaner resumed sweeping up and the manager went for a walk, past the car. He mentally took note of the car registration number and walked on. He stopped for a moment to light a cigarette because hanging from the back of the car was a price ticket. As I've said earlier, shops at that time always removed price tags for their records when items were sold. The manager walked on round the block to his own front door and phoned the police. While he was doing so the two women returned to the car again with bulging bags and got into the car, which drove away.

The police traced the car number to a couple living in London, known thieves, so a call went out to every police car. Only about four minutes elapsed before a call came back to the police station. The car was coming to the railway station. The police officer at the station saw two women get out of the car and make for the trains. He saw the man get ready to drive away, so he went over to him and stopped him. The policeman said he wanted the man to open the boot of his car, which he did quite willingly. The police officer saw it was full of clothes and other items.

When asked about them, the man said, "I'm a traveller and they are my samples."

Well! The police officer could find no labels, and the man had a list of all the items in the boot.

By this time three other panda cars had arrived and the question arose: should the police officer insist the man came back to the police station? After all, no one had seen the man or even the women actually take the things. Perhaps they were a legitimate lot of samples and the women were his sales staff.

Anyway, the police officer said, "What train did your two ladies catch?"

The man denied all knowledge of the two ladies, except that he had given them a lift. He said they couldn't find a cab to get them to the station in time for their train. When asked where he'd picked them up he said, "In the town centre."

On radioing this news to headquarters, the police officer was told to bring the man and the car in.

On checking the train timetable the police ascertained that only the London train left at that time. A search was made of the station, but the two ladies seemed to have caught the train.

The man was driven in his car to the police station. He stuck to his story of being a traveller, although the police felt sure he was lying. They searched his car thoroughly, but could find nothing to prove the goods were stolen.

A phone call came through to the police station saying that the ladies' cloakroom attendant had found a bag in the Ladies containing a lot of torn-up price tickets. She had known the police were looking for two ladies and wondered if there was any connection. A police car went and collected the bag, and – do you know? – the bag was identical to the description given by the cleaner to the police. The woman who went to the car had taken clothes out of a similar bag.

The London police were alerted to stop the two women when they got off the train. The police, having recognized one of our jackets, had sent for me and here I was now to identify the goods. I spent the best part of the next hour piecing our price tickets together. Having done so, I selected the clothes that they belonged to from the pile and gradually we sorted it all out. Quite a lot of the stuff was not ours, and various other store detectives were called in. Soon it was quite a party, each girl identifying the things that belonged to her shop. Dutifully we wrote our statements, and while doing so a call came through from the London police to say they had stopped the two women. When asked if they had come from our town both women denied having been here. In fact, their tickets said they had come from a town some hour and a half further from London than we were. Anyway our police went and collected the two women, who were kept by the London police until our lads arrived.

In the meantime we were chatting – that is, our local police officers and the other store detectives. Having sorted out what clothes and goods belonged to what shop there was still quite a pile of unclaimed items, and none of us could think which shop they could belong to. I happened to say that one of our assistants must have had her eyes shut, because she remembered putting a customer into a fitting room with the yellow and the lilac swimsuits.

"In fact these," I said, showing the two that were now here in the police station. "The stupid girl then forgot about the customer until I made enquiries about six black-and-white swimsuits, which had somehow disappeared." And again I pointed, to six black-and-white swimsuits still on their hangers in the pile. I continued: "All the assistant can remember is the amethyst ring one of the women wore on her right hand."

With that, a detective constable said, "Can she describe it?"
I said, "Yes."

Off went the Detective Constable and I to get a description of the ring. The assistant was a bit nervous, but gave a complete description of the ring and off went a happy detective constable.

It was now past closing time, so off I went home. Next day I discovered what had happened.

At seven thirty that evening the police and the two women had arrived back at our police station and the interviews began. Both women absolutely denied knowing the man, or having been to our town that day. As far as the clothes were concerned they'd never seen them in their lives. In fact, they said, "Some of them aren't even our size."

Anyway, after about half an hour of these denials, the detective constable who had taken the statement from our assistant about the ring said to the lady concerned, "You were in the store today at 11 a.m. You took a yellow and a lilac swimsuit into a fitting room. That was the last time those two items were seen in the store."

The lady said, "You're mistaken. I have not been in that shop or this town today and you can't prove it."

The Detective Constable took from his now quite considerable pile of statements the one made out by our assistant relating to the ring and the lady. He showed it to her and then took her right hand from under the desk, where it had suddenly shot. The Detective Constable said, "I suggest that your ring has been beautifully described by the assistant."

The woman said, "I want a solicitor."

"By all means," said the Detective Constable, and moved a phone towards her.

"Oh, all right," said the woman, "but she made me do it" – referring to the other woman – "and the man's her brother."

After a lot more sorting out the police discovered that the goods not claimed by any of us had in fact been stolen from Norwich, the town where the two women had their train tickets from when stopped by the police in London. They had gone from London the previous day to Norwich, where they had done some shoplifting. They then got a train as far as us and were met by the man, who gave them platform tickets. They did their shoplifting in our town, and returned to London by getting into the station using their platform tickets and then using their original tickets to continue their journey to London. The man had been with them at both places to carry the loot in his car. As he had not been in the shops, he thought he was safe. He would have been but for the cleaner and the sales assistant.

You see, even if we super detectives miss a good professional gang, as these were, someone is likely to see something; and if all the heads are put together, a good fair cop is made. A week later they were all fined – the man £75 and the two women £50 each – at the local magistrates' court, and high praise was given to the cleaner.

I think all we detectives felt a little ashamed of ourselves because every day, for about three weeks after, a shoplifter was caught in one of our shops by one of us. We wanted to be sure we were kept on the payroll of our respective shops.

I am unable to relate any tales of thieves that actually did get away without my noticing them, because as I didn't notice them I can't describe them. I'm sure there must have been quite a few. As I've said so often, sometimes shoplifters get away with it several times before they get caught; but any people who got away with it in my store I hope got caught elsewhere eventually.

TWO PARTICULAR SHOPLIFTERS AND THE CONSEQUENCES

By the time I had been with the store for about five years I was usually catching two people a week – more just before Christmas. I was respected by the staff and management and they often said what a good job I was doing. However, no one knew that every time I saw a shoplifter I still felt the same as I did that morning when I saw Mrs A take the table lamp five years before. I don't suppose I will ever get over the shock of seeing someone steal.

In our town during June, July and August we had about 2,000 students from different countries learning English. There were Japanese, Chinese, French, Italians, Spaniards – oh, practically every nationality – and I'm afraid to say that many of them thought our English shops fair game. It didn't really matter much if they got caught because the offence was dealt with by the local magistrates and usually it was a fine. As they often had a lot of money with them they were able to pay the fine without much hardship; then off they went home at the end of their course and Mama and Papa at home never knew.

Anyway, one beautiful July afternoon I was standing by our front doors. They'd been flung wide open because it was quite warm. My attention was drawn to a beautiful, young, olive-skinned girl. She really was lovely to look at. She was wearing a very fine pink cotton dress and white rope sandals – the ones that tie just below the knee. She carried a white purse-type bag. She had a lovely diamond ring on her right hand and a tiny gold watch on her left wrist. I was standing admiring this slim girl as she looked at our display of small leather goods. She was looking at a brown crocodile wallet – quite expensive it was. (I knew most of the prices of our goods by this time.) The young lady looked around her, opened her bag and put the wallet in. Then she started to move away, but she suddenly stopped and returned.

'Gosh!' I said to myself. 'It's perfectly all right – she's now going to pay for it.'

I stood at the side of her and again she was examining the crocodile wallets. I relaxed. I thought she must be wondering which was the best buy, but she had not as yet brought the first one out of her handbag. I wondered why. Then she picked up another two crocodile wallets and began moving away again. Oh no!

By this time I had regained my lost composure and felt quite cross. What a cool customer – simply helping herself! Yes, here we go again, only this time two wallets went into the bag and I felt like shouting, "Now there are three." But of course I kept my distance and her under observation.

We slowly ambled through the shop and eventually out of the front doors. As she left the shop, for some reason I noticed two young olive-skinned men on the other side of the road, but they seemed to be of no consequence so I went quickly up to the girl and said, "You speak English?"

She said, "Yes."

I said, "Please come back. You have not paid for the wallets in your bag."

I suddenly knew those two men opposite were something to do with the girl. They were watching us very closely. I decided I had to get her back inside very quickly. The traffic between them and us was quite heavy, but I could see they were trying to cross.

I said to the girl, "Come back now."

She came quite willingly, but I fairly pulled her through the shoppers to the manager's office. As usual the secretary jumped out of her seat and we were quickly ushered into the office. I don't think I have ever been so glad to be in that office before or since.

I got on with the job and told the manager, "I saw this young lady take a wallet from the display and as she walked away put it into her bag. She returned, took two more and again put them into her bag."

The manager said to the girl, "Is this true?"

She replied, "Yes, and I will pay you now." With that she opened her bag and took out three wallets, also her own fat purse/wallet, and said, "Take what is necessary."

The manager and I looked, without touching, at her purse bulging with money. (Later, at the police station, I learnt it contained £502 16s. 4d.) The manager said the police were to be called.

The girl said, "Will they cut my fingers off?"

Apparently in her country that is what they did to thieves – you must remember this all happened more than forty years ago.

The police took the girl to the police station and enquiries were made about her. When I visited the station to make my statement I was told she was the daughter of an extremely wealthy family and she was here studying English for four months. She was in a suite all to herself in our poshest hotel. She had her own staff, including maid, food taster (in case of poisoning) and chauffeur. The latter was English and had been hired for the duration of her stay; there appeared to be one or two others, but the police didn't know what jobs they did.

The police said, "She's been in touch with her father's solicitor and it appears it's going to be a Crown Court job – no small stuff in the magistrates' court for them; the best legal defence from London for her. She says she was not thinking when she put the wallets into her own bag. She thought it was her own wallet."

I left the police station and off I went home. It was now five thirty. I told my husband about it and thought no more.

Next morning I caught my usual bus, chatted to the usual passengers, got off the bus and went into the store. I went to the manager's office and explained what I'd learnt at the police station the evening before. I then went on to the shop floor. I did my duty, though I did not catch anybody, then at my usual time I went for my bus home. I waited (as usual it was late). Eventually it came. I got on and so did a young olive-skinned man!

I must have been reading too many police stories or watching too many *Z Cars* programmes or something, because, as I've said, there are many students in our town in July; but he worried me. Was I being followed? I got off at my stop, which is the last one on that journey. The young man was still on the bus, so he too had to get off. My house was only about twelve houses from the stop, so I quickly entered and shut the door behind me. I ran upstairs and peeped through my net curtains at the man. He walked at a very leisurely pace up the road and round the corner. Daft me – the job was getting on top of me. I was a twit.

I got the tea and forgot the incident. My children told me of their activities and the evening passed.

All too soon it was the next morning, Saturday. On Saturdays Ron took me to work in the car. He dropped me off and picked up his parents; then he took them to our house for the day. This way he didn't have to get a midday meal for himself and the kids – his mother did it. I think and hope she enjoyed being with her son and grandchildren. Anyway, this Saturday as we passed my normal bus stop I glanced across and there, sitting on the low wall at the bus stop, was the olive-skinned young man. I started to shake from head to toe.

I knew that if I said anything to my husband, he'd either say I had a vivid imagination or, "That's it – no more work for you." And I really wasn't sure I was being followed. After all, it was quite possible that the young man lived nearby and was just going to work or town.

Ron asked me if I would I go to Boots and get him something during the day.

I said, "No – I am sorry, but I won't have time."

I thought if I stayed in the shop all day, I'd be safe. Ron was picking me up in the evening and dropping me there that morning, so I thought I'd just keep an open mind but play it safe. I must admit I was quite worried.

I went into the store and started to wander around. At ten thirty I went for my coffee and a ham roll in our super canteen. At ten forty-five I dutifully returned to the shop and wandered around. In the customer restaurant I saw him. Our eyes met and I knew I was being followed. I plucked up courage and went to see the manager. I told him about the young man and that he was now in our restaurant. The manager called the police. When they arrived I told them what had been happening, but by the time the police went to the restaurant he had gone.

The police said under no circumstances was I to go anywhere alone. I was to come to work in a police car and return home the same way, unless my husband could meet me.

I was then asked about my children. The manager of our store was very kind and said the firm would pay for my children to be taken to school by taxi and returned by taxi. The police advised me not to stay in my house alone or let the children be there alone.

Ron collected me after I'd finished work that Saturday evening, and on the way home I explained to him and the children what was going on. Of course the kids thought it super fun, but Ron was extremely worried.

On the Sunday we went to the coast for the day. It poured with rain all day, but we enjoyed our fish and chips and forgot the olive-skinned man.

On Mondays I never worked; it was my day off. The taxi took the children to school. I kept peering through the net curtains. My cleaning lady came and we did some clearing-up. There was no sign of the olive-skinned man.

On Tuesday a panda car turned up after the taxi and off I went to work. There was no sign of my olive-skinned man that day; nor was there that week. After consultation with the police at the end of the week, with nothing happening, I returned to my usual routine on the bus; and although the children had the taxi for the second week I didn't see the young man again until two months later in the Crown Court, where the young lady appeared on the charge of theft of the three wallets. Apparently he was one of her bodyguards.

After I had spoken to the police about being followed they had been to see the young lady because they had felt it might be something to do with her. She admitted that she'd asked the young man to try to give me some money to say I'd made a mistake, but the young man never got the opportunity of speaking quietly to me. The police warned her to keep him and any of her other guards away from me or they'd stick her in prison, That was why I didn't see the young man again until the court case.

Now, I'd never been to a Crown Court case before and I was very nervous. There's a judge, twelve honest men and women, various other officials of the court, the defendant (in this case, the young girl, who sat in the box with a very large woman prison officer on either side of her), her barrister wearing his powdered wig and our prosecuting solicitor. Quite soon I was called to give my evidence. I told the court how I'd watched the young lady take the wallet, walk away and put it in her bag, and she did it a second time with the two wallets.

Her barrister said Miss — in her evidence will say she thought it was her own wallet that she was putting away into her bag. What do you say about that? I replied that maybe on the first occasion she did think it was her own wallet, but how could she possibly have thought that on the second time round, when it was in fact two wallets she was pushing away one after the other? If I've got one thing, it doesn't suddenly divide into two for me to put away.

Anyway, after a lot more questions and speeches the jury left the room to come back with the verdict: "We find the case proven."

In other words, she was guilty. The judge then fined her £30 and we all went home.

Another shoplifter I want to tell you about was a lady of some thirty-eight years, who in fact lived in the next road to mine. I had been at my store about four years when this incident took place. The lady was single, but her son of about twenty-one years lived with her. Before I stopped her I did not know her, but I had read in our local evening paper several times of her son's exploits.

Let me start at the beginning. It was coming up towards Christmas. It was cold outside, and on that particular day there had been several flurries of snow. I was upstairs in the linen department – I was hoping to get a boxed pillowcase set for an aunt's Christmas present – when I saw a tall, gaunt woman just standing looking at items on display and also looking at the staff. She was standing in front of a tabletop display of cushion covers. She appeared to like a rose-patterned cushion cover. She kept picking it up and putting it down. Every time it went down it was folded a little bit more. The first time it was in half, the second time in quarters and then it was rolled up. She picked it up again, and as she turned away it went into her coat pocket. She looked all round her and then very slowly she ambled away from the department. I followed. Downstairs she went, out of the front door with me following.

"Excuse me, madam. I am the store detective from this store and you've left without paying for the cushion cover in your right pocket."

"Oh dear – have I?" said the woman. "I must have forgotten."

I said, "Please come to the manager's office."

"Of course, my dear," said the woman.

So off we trailed to the office, past the secretary and in to see the manager. The police were called and that, I thought, was that.

I went to make my statement to the police as usual, but I was greeted with, "You know what you've done?"

I looked blank.

"You caught Miss W. Last time she was caught her son set fire to the store detective's car. He threw a cigarette in through a window that was slightly open."

"Oh well," I said, "I haven't got a car."

"No," they said, "but they only live round the corner from you."

"Oh!" said I.

The young man had only just come out of prison after serving a six-month sentence for arson. The police advised me to keep everything locked at home and to alert my neighbours. I was to tell them that if they should see anyone not known to them, particularly a young man, around my house, they were to call the police immediately. The police did feel that I and my house would be safe. The young man had only just come out and they had warned his mother that if anything happened to the store detective or her belongings, they would know whom to pick up.

After catching Miss W, and fearing possible consequences, I began to wonder about the future. Should I continue with the job? But what else could I do? I was a trained nursery nurse, but I did not want to be with children because I felt that if one has children it is a bit of a bore to have children all day and then come home in the evening and still have to listen to children. As it was now, my job involved grown-ups and listening to my children was fresh to me in the evening. But what was I to do? I certainly didn't want anything to happen to my house or children. Were my children getting a wrong outlook on life? They were growing up and were always interested in my cases. Perhaps I was giving them a jaundiced look at life. After so many years of watching people and waiting for them to pinch, and so many of them did, I was tired of it all. Many days I went to work and spent the entire day hiding in the staff loos. There were eight in all and I would spend three-quarters of an hour in each. Some days I would force myself out on to the floor, and it was one of those spells that finished me completely.

It is not only customers that pinch; the staff too are not always honest. So special customers who belong to a security organization come into the store and purchase items and watch to see that the assistant does in actual fact put the money in the till. A lot of people will say that's not fair. Staff are generally honest – yes, I'll agree – but occasionally a crooked person is taken on and instead of putting customers' money in the till she puts it in her pocket. If the department finds the till is always short, everyone on that till will be suspected; so it is much better for the thief to be caught.

However, one day I was on the shop floor, having forced myself out of the loos, and I noticed two young ladies comparing notes at the top of the stairs. I really don't know why I noticed them, but I did. They went down the stairs to the hardware department, and I followed. They purchased some small items and I wondered whether they were the professional shoppers from the security organization. I followed, they then went their separate ways and I stayed with the blonde one. She walked around and eventually she went to a display of belts. She worried me. She was constantly looking about her. Perhaps she wanted to 'test-purchase' a particular assistant. My God! She had just put a belt from the display into her pocket. She obviously couldn't have been with the security firm. I don't know why, but I was sure she was. Anyway, she walked away with the belt in her pocket; she made no attempt to pay for it. She wandered over to the boxes of handkerchiefs, picked up two, dropped them into her own bag, stood for a few minutes and then shot out of the shop.

I raced after her and said, "I'm from the store and you've left with a belt and some boxed handkerchiefs you've not paid for."

Very coolly she said, "Oh, yes! I must make up my notes."

I said, "Are you from —?" and named the security firm.

She replied, "Yes. I must do my notes."

For five minutes I stood with her. Eventually I said, "Please come with me to the office."

She said, "No. I've only been test-purchasing."

I said, "Please come and explain that to the manager."

I had by now caught hold of her arm and was gently pushing her towards the door. Two of my store's male assistants had noticed I'd run out of the store and not come back, so they came out and were able to move my lady inside the shop for me. I felt awful. Of all the hypocritical things to do, that woman was testing our staff and pinching at the same time. I felt sick through to my stomach.

I went to the manager with her and told him everything, including the fact that she had been testing our staff. He too was disgusted.

Of course she lost her job with her firm and went to court and was fined £30, but I remember I had to have a taxi home. I'd had more than enough.

For a further year I took driving lessons. I passed my test, much to the amazement of my driving instructor, and still continued to go to work. My number of apprehensions was certainly declining. Then I saw a job advertised for a mail-order rep – company car provided. I applied and got the job. I gave up being a store detective. I told everyone that was it – no more snooping and no more tensions. Oh, I felt so relieved.

I was a mail-order rep for three years; then we moved and I did not work for a year.

A NEW JOB

Then I saw advertised in our local paper, 'Chief Security Officer required to organise a security branch for our shops and stores.' I applied and got the job. Two days after the interview I started work.

Never having had a proper security team, this firm didn't know what was about to hit them.

I visited every shop belonging to them – about sixty in all. I didn't let the staff know who I was – not even the managers. I made a report on all the shops simply for myself.

I then introduced myself to the manager of one of the largest shops and said, "I'll catch some shoplifters."

Remember, I'd not done any security work for four years so I was a bit rusty. I wandered around and saw nothing for two weeks. With this firm I was full-time, so I couldn't even blame the fact no shoplifters were apprehended on the possibility that shoplifting took place when I wasn't at work. I was there from nine until five.

After two weeks the management, whom I had convinced at my interview that I was good at catching thieves, must have been wondering what I was doing. Then at ten o'clock on a Tuesday morning I saw a lad in the ladies' underwear department take and put into his bag a suspender belt. Hurrah, a shoplifter! All the old feelings came back – cement in my shoes, bashing heart... Anyway, I followed him, stopped him outside and brought him back to the office. A very hectic session had started.

Two hours later I followed a man out of the shop, tapped him on the shoulder and said, "I am the security—" and he raced down the road.

I was quite taken aback. He was gone. I returned to the shop and alerted the police. I had forgotten the police didn't know me. I had to start to get to know the police again.

I had seen this man in the menswear department. He had been looking around him. I had a funny feeling about him, but he was not carrying a bag or anything else. He selected three pairs of jeans, asked an assistant if he could try them on and went into a fitting room. Twice he peeped out through the curtains. When the assistant was busy the man came out of the fitting room and put two pairs back on the hangers. He was now carrying a carrier bag containing something – the third pair of jeans. Very quickly he left the department and went out of the shop, and then I tried to stop him. I should have grabbed the bag, but didn't.

I had to start to get to know the police again. After all the years away, most of the police I knew had been promoted or moved elsewhere and I had to get to know the new ones. They all seemed to me to be so young. One of the CID officers remembered me and we had a fine old chat. I was shown the bad boys' book, but I was unable to pick out my runaway man.

I returned to the shop. The manager was quite chatty. I felt relieved that I'd started to catch thieves. I even got a cup of tea in the manager's office.

I returned to the shop floor and twenty minutes later a lady in a mock-leopard-skin-type mac came into the shop. Vaguely I remembered seeing her before somewhere. It didn't bother me, but I kept an eye on her. She picked up a bottle of Tweed perfume, looked at it and quietly slipped it into her pocket. She proceeded to look at lipsticks. Her fingers folded round one and she moved away, still holding it. She continued to walk around the shop and then she walked out of the shop. I followed her outside.

I went up to her and said, "Excuse me, madam. You have just left the store without paying for a Tweed perfume and a lipstick."

Absolutely dumbfounded, the woman said, "Oh yes!"

She did give me such funny looks that I wondered if there was anything odd about me. However, we got back to the office. I told the manager the circumstances and we called the police. I took the lady's name and address and off they went to the police station.

About one hour later I went to the police station again. Now I was able to go by car – my own – whereas I had had to walk before at my first job, and often arrived all hot and bothered. Now I arrived cool and elegant – no falling on my face, as with my first shoplifter.

Anyway, I made my statement at the police station. The policeman read it through and said, "Do you remember her?" referring to the shoplifter I'd just caught.

I said, "Well, I've seen her before somewhere."

He said, "You caught her six years ago at the other shop you worked at."

I was truly amazed. When I got home I looked at all the papers I had kept and found the case. Yes, I had caught her at the other shop stealing a necklace and a lipstick. I think that when she was looking at me a bit funnily she was trying to remember where she'd seen me before.

My goodness, on returning to the shop the manager was so nice! They had never had three in one day – even if one had got away. Was I in! I there and then decided to visit another shop the next day. I was not likely to keep up three a day and I thought I'd have a better chance of getting one where I was not known.

My new firm also had food shops, and I found catching people in these shops very difficult. I had been used to seeing larger items stolen, so a quick slip of the hand into the pocket with a tin of salmon took a bit of getting used to. However, I worked at it and now find food shoplifters very easy to spot.

I made quite a number of arrests and was beginning to feel acknowledged as a good store detective by my new firm. As I have said, the firm had never had its own security team and they were truly amazed at the amount of thieving I was beginning to show was going on.

I made several staff arrests. The first staff theft I discovered was in a small grocery shop situated in a village seven miles from our main offices. I went to this shop on a Thursday just to have a look around. I was just like any other shopper getting my groceries in a wire basket. I saw a staff member put a full wire basket on the floor under a fixture. She then went to the checkout operator and bought 200 cigarettes, a bottle of wine and a box of chocolates. She paid and got her receipt. She walked back to her wire basket, picked it up and went out through the staff doors to the back of the shop. I was not certain, so I could do nothing. She might have been getting an order for a customer, but I was suspicious about the way she held the receipt in front of the goods for everyone to see, as if she was saying, "Look – I've paid. Here's the receipt." I paid for my groceries and left the shop. No one knew who I was.

The following Thursday at exactly the same time I entered the shop and immediately saw the staff member collecting items into a wire basket: fish fingers, horseradish sauce, a lettuce, sugar, tea, coffee, margarine, butter, a packet of dried peas, a packet of biscuits, and some pre-packed cheese and bacon. The basket was then placed on the floor under the fixture and off she went to the checkout operator. I was immediately after her in the queue. I heard her ask for 200 cigarettes, a bottle of wine (red this week; it had been white the previous week) and a pound box of Dairy Milk chocolates. In all it came to £6.02. She paid and got her receipt. I was then served, but I was able to watch her pick up her wire basket and, again holding the receipt in front of her, she went through the staff doors. I paid for my items and went to the rear of the shop, where my car was parked in the car park. I got in and watched the staff member putting all the groceries from the wire basket into her bicycle basket and bag at the back. She covered it all up then went inside. At noon she came out carrying a shopping bag. It was her lunch hour.

I approached her and, showing my identity card, I said, "I wish to check your purchases against your receipt."

She said, "Oh yes, here it is," and she took the receipt from her purse and handed it to me. Of course in her shopping bag were 200 cigarettes, a bottle of wine and a box of chocolates.

I said, "Thank you. That's fine, but I want the receipt for the groceries in your bike basket and bag."

She sort of swallowed and said, "I'll pay this afternoon when I come back."

I said, "Do you always pay in the afternoon for goods taken in the morning?"

"No, I've never done it before. I'm in a hurry today," she said.

I said, "What about last week?"

She lost her voice completely and was struck dumb.

We went back to the manager and the lady was sacked. The manager was amazed that he had never even suspected such a thing could have been going on under his nose. I think he was annoyed with me because it made him look as if he was not doing his job properly in the chief's eyes at Head Office, and he was always a bit frosty with me after that.

During the next year I caught several shoplifters in his shop and also another member of his staff who used to take half a pound of ham in her handbag every evening. However, the thing that made him even more frosty with me resulted from the following. Since my first encounter with him almost eighteen months had gone by and I had been joined by another security officer, whom I shall call Sally. Head Office had requested that I should check the purchases made by managers as they left their shops. It was a good example to ordinary staff that managers were also checked up on. Anyway, Sally and I went to this shop especially to check this manager. We arrived at twelve fifty-five on a Saturday. The shop was closed after one o'clock. I borrowed my husband's car. I got an allowance from the firm to run a car – as I was doing about 500 miles a week we had decided I should have my own – but because I had borrowed Ron's car the manager didn't know it was me waiting outside. He knew my car.

Sally and I sat outside the front of the shop. It was a difficult shop to watch. As I've said, there is a car park at the rear, but there are two exits for cars. Both come out into the High Street: one (a very open one) between our shop and a butchers, and the other up a very narrow unmade lane. A large empty house stood on the other side of the lane from our shop and tall elder trees overhung the entire lane. It was a very creepy, spooky place even in the middle of the day. The staff left the shop and all went quiet. Sally looked through the windows (she was not known), and yes, the manager was still in the shop. She then went and stood by the open exit and I went to the lane exit. Everywhere became deserted. Sally stood and I stood. Then it started to snow. It was now one thirty and we were frozen. Where on earth was the manager? We could stand it no longer, so we got into the car. Whatever was he doing? Ah! The lights were going out. By now we both felt sick, with very wobbly legs. Oh dear, let's go home. Why are we doing this job? We both had a Polo to calm our nerves. Our hearts were like a pair of tom-toms. Surely someone would hear!

At last, out came the manager. He looked around him and locked the front doors. He tried the doors again. He looked at my car. Sally and I both ducked, but unfortunately we were not far away from each other and, oh boy, did our heads collide! Smash! But duty calls.

The manager started to walk to the rear of the shop, where I knew his car was parked. I started the engine to follow him and stop him as he got into his car. I was a nervous cold wreck with a thumping head. I slammed the car into gear, but unfortunately it was reverse. In my husband's car, reverse is in the position of first gear in my car. I braked after getting a bit near a wall. Then, with terrific concentration, I found first and we were off; but those few minutes messing about were enough for the manager to get into his car and lock a gate behind him. Now he had started to go down the lane towards the High Street. I quickly turned the car and raced round to the lane exit, so we met nose to nose.

Sally got out one side and I the other. We went up to him and I said, "Hallo. You know who I am, don't you?"

He seemed petrified. I've never seen anyone go so grey and shake. His teeth were chattering. Sally looked at me. We both could smell his fear. Here, we thought, was a manager with a boot full of goods. I could see there was nothing inside the car.

"Will you please open your boot?"

Swallowing hard and coughing, he squeaked, "Yes."

He turned his engine off, staggered out of the car and opened the boot. Nothing – not a single packet of crisps! Nothing at all!

I politely said, "Thank you."

He got into his car and lit a cigarette, his hands still shaking dreadfully. Sally and I got into my car. We backed out and drove away. What had happened? We couldn't understand it. He had been petrified when we stopped him, but why? Had he had things stuffed under his car seats? Surely if he was stealing, there would have been no need to hide things because this was one of the first checks we'd done on a manager; but he was so frightened. Why?

About ten days later I found out why. A person employed in the office told me, "You scared the pants right off Michael, didn't you?" and he laughed.

I said, "Well, who is Michael?"

"You know," he said. "You did a check on him at his shop in — village."

Intrigued, I said, "Everything was in order. He did seem to be frightened, though."

He said, "Michael thought you were robbers. Usually he carries the cash with him on Saturdays. This week he had put it in the post office nearby. He honestly thought as you raced round the corner just as he was leaving that you were after the money. He told me he was trapped. He had locked the gate behind him, everywhere was quiet and this sports car that he didn't recognize came roaring round the corner, two doors flew open and out got two persons. He honestly thought it was a hold-up. If he'd had a gun, he'd have shot you, he was so petrified. He didn't recognize you until you spoke, and even then he was shaking so he said nothing. Ha ha!"

Sally, when I told her, laughed herself silly. We agreed we thought he'd think twice about pinching goods – not that we have any reason to think he ever did.

NEW STAFF FOR ME

Let me tell you how the ladies who work with me joined me. The firm was so delighted with the work I was doing that when I said I really wanted help they advertised in the local papers. I interviewed several ladies, but didn't like them. I knew one store detective, Sally, who was good, but she was working for another firm. Several times I asked her to join me, but she was happy where she was. She was very good at her job and I felt we could work well together. She only wanted part-time work. I spoke to my boss, who agreed that she could work part-time, but again she said no.

I had had a tip-off that a manageress in a very small shop of ours was taking money from customers and not putting it into the till. She knew who I was, so I asked Sally if she would go and buy an item from the woman. I could see the till from outside. Sally made a purchase and everything was rung up. As we stood talking outside a man went in and purchased an item for £4.35 and only thirty-five pence was rung up on the till. Hurrah – we had her!

I approached the customer as he left the shop and I said, "I see you've just made a purchase from this shop."

He replied, "Yes."

I said, "I work for the firm and we are finding out if customers are pleased with their purchases and if they have any comments to make."

He said, "No."

I said, "How much was your purchase?"

He said, "£4.35."

I said, "Did you get a receipt?"

He said, "Oh, no – I suppose I should have done. I'll go and get it."

Sally started to giggle. Imagine him returning to the shop and asking for his receipt! All would have been lost.

"No, sir," said I. "It is irrelevant whether you have a receipt or not. We are just interested to have your opinion of the service we try to give."

"Fine," he said and went to his car.

He gave us a funny look and drove off. I took his car number in case when we called the police he was needed to give evidence. I even got that wrong: it was something V something, and in my haste at the police station I told them something U something. Several times they were told that no such number existed; however, when they tried something V something the police learnt the car owner lived just around the corner from the shop. However, he was never called to give evidence. The woman admitted taking £2,000 over the years from the firm.

Two years after this incident the flat roof of my garage at home was leaking. In the *Yellow Pages* I found a flat-roof expert and he agreed to come and do it for me. The next evening he drove up my drive and yes, believe it or not, it was the something-V-something car and the driver was the man I had spoken to. I dived into the house and my husband dealt with him.

I do wander about. Back to Sally. Even after the excitement of catching a big one she was still reluctant to join me. One day when I was at a village police station making a statement about a shoplifter I'd caught, a phone call came through to the Sergeant.

"No, dear, I can't find anything suitable," said the Sergeant, and then he rambled on. Eventually he replaced the phone. "That was a young lady I know who wants to find a job in this area," he said to me. "She's at present in charge of the secretarial department at a large police station, and she's moving this way with her husband. Her father's a very high-ranking police officer and she started here as a junior in my office – such a nice young lady."

"Oh," said I, "what about her becoming a store detective for me?" I continued: "I'm looking for someone in this area. Does she drive?"

"Yes."

"Here's my phone number. Tell her to contact me if she fancies the job."

That evening at home Janet phoned me. She was willing to have a go. I said I'd arrange an interview for her.

Before I was able to do so Sally phoned me and said, "I've made up my mind: I'll join you."

Now I was in a predicament. I had almost promised the job to Janet, feeling sure Sally wouldn't leave her own job. I went to my chief and explained what had happened.

"Well," said he, "if you like them, we'll take both on."

So Sally and Janet joined me. Sally started one month before Janet as she didn't need training. I was with her for her first week only, introducing her to various managers and senior staff. Janet, never having done the job before, needed to be completely trained. I took her everywhere for a month and we did not see one small shoplifting offence. I tried so hard to find a shoplifter so Janet could see how we went about things. Anyway, the first one we did catch I had seen and Janet had not. I'd seen a very pregnant lady push two plates from the display into her shopping bag. She was with a friend. She also took a small box of twenty teaspoons. As they were leaving the shop Janet and I followed them out. I stopped the pregnant lady and told her who I was.

She pushed at me and then said, "If you touch my bag, I'll wrap it round your — neck."

After a bit of a struggle we all returned to the manager's office. Janet was first class, although scared stiff, she told me afterwards. She didn't panic and I was glad of her help to get the two women back.

About a month later the case went to court and we learnt that the pregnant woman had had her child since the offence and it had been immediately taken away from her because she had murdered two she had previously had, one at eighteen months and the other at two years of age. She was a right bad lot. She didn't turn up for the court case. A warrant was issued for her arrest, but she still hadn't been found two years later.

If either Sally or Janet ever read this, I would like them to know what a pleasure it was to work with both of them. In the larger stores of our company we would often work together, and we became known as 'Charlie's Angels' after the three TV lady detectives. Janet was the dark one, slim, young and pretty. Sally and I – well, I'm older than Sally by a few years, but we were both past thirty-five years (she'll kill me for that) and we could never work out which of the Angels we were. Of course none of us carried a gun in our stocking top.

We were joined by a fourth young lady. Her husband was a police officer.

I must try to describe to you some of the antics we got up to when trying to catch thieving staff members. Having been with the company a number of years, we were all quite well known by the staff. I was useless at dressing up in disguises, but Sally – well, words fail me! She was superb. She normally wore rather thick glasses, but she frequently changed the colour of her hair, though never to black.

One day we drove sixty miles to one of our stores where we knew a staff member was not putting customers' money into the till, but into her own pocket. When we arrived at our destination I drove to the town multistorey car park and parked. Sally began her transformation. First she put on a short, straight black wig; she then took off her glasses and we went into hysterics as she proceeded to put her contact lenses into her eyes. Janet and I had never seen anything like it before, both having normal sight. She opened her left eye with her fingers and with a tiny, tiny 'plunger' popped a lens in. She then blinked furiously. She happened to glance to the left of her and a man sitting in his car was transfixed, watching her.

There were more peals of helpless laughter, then an anguished "Shut up, you two" from Sally. "I think I've lost it in the tears of laughter." There was more furious blinking. "I can't see a damn thing." We controlled ourselves and Sally said, "I think it's still in. Is there someone in the car at the side of me?"

She couldn't, or daren't, turn round, but I looked past her and the man was rubbing his eyes. He probably couldn't believe his eyes.

Anyway, Sally then found her right lens in its little case and popped it in.

She said, "My eyes will stop running in about ten minutes."

We sat in silence, eating some ham rolls, until her eyes calmed down. All was soon well and she continued with her heavy make-up. She looked so different. Then she put on an old coat and off she went to make her purchase.

Janet and I waited at the entrance to the car park and after half an hour had elapsed Sally fairly hopped along the road. We knew she'd done it! The girl has pocketed the money. Sally told us that twice she had bought something from the girl and twice she hadn't rung it up.

I like to have two separate purchases made by different people, so we got Janet to dress up. She hid all her hair inside a woolly hat. She sometimes wears glasses, so she donned them and off she went.

Sally and I returned to the car and the reverse process began. She got her little 'plunger' out and placed it in her eye and out popped a lens. She found the bottle for the left one and then got the other one out and popped that into its own little bottle. I'm afraid I was roaring with laughter again. Sally joined in when she put her glasses on and saw that her wig was crooked. The parting ran across her head instead of from back to front. Fortunately the man in his car at the side of us had gone.

Janet joined us, looking very gloomy. The girl had rung her money up on the till. Anyway, later on that day I questioned the girl and she admitted it.

VARIOUS INCIDENTS

I had a call from a country shop. A young lady was going into this particular shop spending about an hour wandering up and down and eventually leaving with just a loaf or a bag of flour. It was most odd. I was told that she came in every day at coffee time, about nine thirty. She was about twenty-one, with long fair hair. She wore glasses and was about five feet tall.

I had a trainee detective with me, so as this shop was about fifty miles from my home I made arrangements to pick Pat up at her home and said we would be at the shop at nine thirty on Tuesday morning.

"Fine," said the manager.

We duly arrived at nine twenty-five. Immediately I asked the manager if the girl had been in.

"Yes," he said. "She was in yesterday; it's usually about three o'clock she comes in."

Pat and I looked at each other – we'd rushed for nothing!

The manager said he was sure he'd told us to come just before three. Anyway, as we were at the shop we thought we'd stay. Pat, being new, was with me every day anyway. We'd not seen much so I really was banking on seeing this girl steal something.

Pat was wandering round the shop and suddenly she came to me quite pale. "A woman over there has put a box of coffee into her bag."

I hared round and saw that the woman had zipped her bag up. No way was I going to take a chance – I'd not seen it, so I decided to leave it and hope she'd come in again sometime.

We wandered on for a bit, then a woman passed us with two

packets of beefburgers in her basket. On the other side of a display she took them from the basket and shoved them into her bag. Pat was shaking. We continued to watch this woman and she proceeded to pinch a tin of meat, a jar of coffee, jellies and a tin of milk. She paid for the rest of her items and off she went. I shoved Pat out of the door and she stopped the woman.

We all returned to the shop and went into the office. Pat explained to the manager what had happened.

The manager signalled to me to come outside with him. He said, "You've had her before, at our big shop in town. I remember reading about it in the paper. She was fined £60."

I returned to the woman, who was appealing to Pat: "Please let me off, dear," she said. "It's the first time I've ever done this sort of thing. I was tempted by all the things on the shelves. I'm not a bad person. My husband hanged himself when my boy was a baby."

Pat appeared to be sympathizing, and I said, "How old is your son now?"

"Thirty-eight," she said.

I butted in: "Have you finished paying your fine from last time?"

She said, "No, and this time I'll go to bloody prison. I'm not paying another fine. I've had to pinch me food to pay it."

With that all her soft, simple niceness disappeared and she sat puffing on a cigarette. The police arrived and off she went with them.

Pat and I continued to walk around the shop. At one o'clock it closed, so we went into the nearby town for dinner. I parked the car and, as we were crossing a road to a café, who should cross in front of us but the woman we had caught earlier. She was quite chirpy, laughing with a friend. We fled.

We returned to the shop at two thirty. We waited and waited, but the girl didn't come in. We went home.

The following Tuesday Pat wanted to see if her coffee woman came in again, so we got to the shop at nine thirty. Sure enough, in came the lady and the coffee went into her bag; but as I was speaking to Pat I think she became suspicious because she took the coffee out of her own bag and hid it among the cornflakes packets. She left the shop.

We wandered around until one o'clock, then as we were going for our dinner I said to the manager, "We'll be back by two thirty."

He said, "I don't think she'll be in; I've not seen her."

I said we'd be back.

We had lunch and returned. We were sitting in the car doing some paperwork, and at the same time we were watching people entering the shop. We noticed a young woman with a child. She had shoulder-length dark hair and was wearing glasses. She was carrying a bag, but we thought nothing of it.

The manager came flying out of the back of the shop and came over to my car. "She's here, she's here," he said.

Pat and I got out of the car and entered the shop. Nothing tied up with our information. The time was two thirty, the girl's hair was dark, and – the biggest mystery – she was accompanied by a child. Anyway, we watched and we saw two bottles of shampoo, two packets of beefburgers, one packet of fish, a large jar of coffee and two packets of bacon disappear into the woman's bag. A few minutes later we confronted her outside the shop, and we all returned, child and all. Pat took the various groceries from the woman's bag and placed them on the table in the manager's office.

The woman refused to say anything, but the child suddenly said, "Mum, Dad will be surprised we're going in a police car again."

Pat and I looked at each other in amazement.

All the woman said was "Shut up."

As we had not mentioned the police it was obvious that the woman had been caught before. Anyway, they did go off in the police car.

About a week later Pat was going home on her bus when who should get on but the lady, the child and a man. Pat was petrified – he looked a real villain. She sat there just hoping everything would be OK.

After about two miles the child looked back at Pat and said, "Mum, there's that lady who was in the shop before we went in the police car."

The man nearly knocked the kid to the floor with "Shut up!" and a biff across the head which petrified Pat even more.

About ten miles further on the man got out of his seat and walked towards Pat. His arm shot up, and Pat ducked, but the man's arm went up to the bell and rang it. They were getting off the bus!

I returned from my holidays in Blackpool, most of which I had spent with my husband and youngest son in the shops. It rained most of the time, so what else could we do but look round the shops? It was a great holiday for me, my working life being spent in shops. However, I returned renewed and refreshed and invigorated with Lancashire sea air.

I went to work at ten o'clock on Tuesday morning – Monday was my day off for that week. I wandered around the shop and found that my shop had fewer exciting things in it than the Blackpool shops had. I got bored and fed up.

I had a coffee at twelve thirty with one of my colleagues. We returned to the shop and wandered in. She went upstairs and I went down. On the ground floor, where I was, were the cosmetics, stationery, footwear, menswear, electrical and record departments. I was walking slowly by the footwear department and a man was walking towards me. I fancied him. He had short, beautifully cut grey/black hair – a lovely-looking man. He had on a beautiful green shirt and darker green trousers. It was a warm day. His shoes were brown and beautifully polished. He had large grey eyes. Here! Here! Here!

'Why is he carrying a ladies' tartan shopping trolley?' I thought. 'His wife will soon arrive, I expect. But no, here comes a second lovely man – a similar type, with grey hair, a grey striped shirt and grey trousers. Immaculate!' The first lovely man went through the exit doors and as they were glass I could see through. The first man put the trolley on the floor and looked back towards the shop; the second lovely man was by now standing inside the doors and looking out. He quickly looked back to where he had come from. He then nodded his head to the first man, who grabbed the trolley and very quickly walked away from the shop. The second man was now joined by a younger man, who although he was smartly dressed was nowhere near as dishy as the other two. He had on a zip-up patterned cardigan and I didn't notice any more except that he did have scruffy brown hair.

I now came to. It dawned on me that they were professionals. What had they got from my shop?

I raced upstairs, grabbed Sally by the arm and said, "Quick – we've just missed our biggest ever."

We raced down the stairs, through the doors, which we left swinging almost off their hinges, and ran up the road to the corner. We screeched to a slow walk round the corner, and there were my three men, walking at the far end of the road to a car park. They went out of sight and we raced down the road. We looked across at the three men, who by now had reached an old car. The first man was in the back of the car with his trolley, and he was doing some odd actions. Eventually he pushed the trolley out to the other two. He appeared to cover something up and then out he got. They locked up the car and off they went towards the other side of the car park and different shops.

Sally followed the men and I went to the car. I very gingerly walked around the car. I tried to appear as if I was looking for my companion. I stood and looked in the window at the back seat; and yes, there was something covered by a blanket. What was it? Had they locked all the doors? I looked around. No one appeared to be interested in me, so I tried the back door. It was locked. I tried the front. It was locked too. By now I was getting braver. I tried the boot. It was locked. So were the other two doors. I carefully wrote the car number and its colour and make in my notebook. By now I really was experienced and I had the necessary equipment for my job – i.e. pen and notebook. I then hared off in the direction Sally had gone, after the men. I must have gone quite quickly because at the entrance to an arcade I found Sally and in front of her I saw the three men looking in a TV/radio shop window. One of the men tried the door and it was shut, so they moved away. The first man still had his trolley. All three men then entered my old shop – the one where I learnt all the tricks of the trade (well, not all, but some; every time I find a shoplifter a new way reveals itself, as shown by that day's theft into a trolley).

Sally and I followed at a discreet distance, straight to the silverware department. A wise shop this one – all the expensive items that had handles were attached to an alarm and all the other items were in glass cases. You should have seen the look of disgust on their faces and their great shaking of heads. They moved round to the menswear department. Sally and I had a discussion. What should we do? Perhaps they were just ordinary shoppers looking for – well, everything or anything. I had not really seen anything. What should I do? What should Sally do? What should we do? They didn't look like criminals. They would be the first shoplifters I fancied – would I fancy a thief? Well, no, but something told me everything was wrong with them.

I made up my mind: Sally should follow the men and I would use the phone and call the police.

As I was known in the shop I quickly said to an assistant, "I want to call the police."

She said, "OK."

I picked up the phone and the switchboard operator said, "Number, please." I gave the police number and the operator said, "Is that our old Mrs Smith?"

Taken aback, I said, "Yes."

"Gosh," she said, "I thought I recognized your voice. The one we got after you left hardly ever caught anyone, so I didn't get to know her very well. What are you doing back?"

I cut in: "Look, dear – get me the police, quick. I've got three shoplifters in your shop."

"Gosh!" she said, and I got my number.

"CID here," a voice said.

"Well," said I, "this is Mrs Smith, security officer. I don't know how to put this, but I think – repeat *think* – three smashing-looking men have pinched something from my shop. I think they are professionals. I'm now at — and they are looking at expensive things, and I'm worried."

The police officer said, "I know you'd like to have one of those men to search, ha ha!"

"Look," said I, "don't be daft. I'm really worried."

"Right," said the policeman, "how soon do you want us?"

I replied, "I'm not sure enough to stop them, but by golly I am worried about them."

"Is two minutes OK?" said the police officer. "I'll meet you outside the shop."

"Fine."

I went to find Sally, and she told me she'd lost sight of all three men. Together we went outside the shop and drawing up in their panda car were a policeman and a policewoman. I told them the story. When the policeman said, "Well, show us the men," I had to say, "We've lost them."

Imagine how I felt. I had seen three men walking out of my shop, go to their car and go into another shop, and now I'd lost sight of them. Where was the great team of professional shoplifters – in my imagination?

"Never mind," said the policeman, "we'll go and have a look at their car." And off they went.

I was not going to be done. Sally went one way round town and I went another. We met and neither of us had seen any of the men.

It was by now two thirty and we were starving hungry. I went to a hot-dog stall and was ordering two hot dogs when I saw the three men walking towards me.

"With onions?" said a voice.

I squeaked, "Yes," and was handed two hot dogs.

The men were passing me, and each of them was licking a cornet ice cream. Sally was frantically signalling to me. I could do nothing to signal back – I had two hot dogs in one hand and my handbag in the other. Anyway, she joined me and we followed the men. They were eating ice cream and we were eating hot dogs. They were lousy hot dogs, but we finished them. The men wandered on and eventually stopped outside a music shop. They looked through the windows; then, after finishing their ice creams, they carefully wiped their hands on snow-white hankies and into the shop they trooped. Sally and I stood up the road a little.

What to do? It was decided that I should follow them into the shop and keep observation. I bravely entered. It was a medium-sized shop with radios in the window for sale. There were also ones in the shop, but those on the shelves had alarm wires attached, unlike the ones in the window. In front of the backless back of the window were large pianos. The three men pulled one of the pianos forward so the first man with his trolley was able to get real close to the back of the window.

The second and third men were talking in very loud voices: "It's so beautiful, so cheap [£796 cheap?]. Do you think it's a little tall for the alcove?"

Out of the second man's pocket came a tape measure. He measured.

"Oh dear," he said, "it's half an inch too tall. What a shame!"

The second man then went to an assistant and the third man went to the only other assistant in the shop. They both spoke in earnest tones to the assistants and the first man took a quick look round.

I was fairly well hidden, looking through a display of tapes. There was no one else in the shop. The two assistants were busy. Up went the first man's hand; down went my stomach to my boots. Up popped a radio/cassette player in the man's hand and oh, so deftly he placed it into the trolley. He quietly closed the lid and lit a cigarette. The other two men joined him and they replaced the piano. Then they smiled at the assistants and out they went, radio/cassette player and all.

I was rooted to the spot. I went to walk out and walked into a pile of record cases and knocked them flying. At this another man appeared. He was the manager.

I showed my identity card and said, "What did you have on display in the window just there?"

"My God," he said, "it's gone – a radio/cassette player worth £59.60."

I told him what I had seen.

"Well, get after them," he said.

"Don't panic," said I. "The police are waiting at their car."

Sally entered the shop and after a few minutes' chit-chat we walked back to the car park.

While we had been trying to find the men around the shops the police had been doing their bit. They had traced the name of the owner of the car and found it was registered at a seaside town about fifty miles away, and the owner had a police record. He was wanted by his local police force for shoplifting, but no one had actually caught him. He 'worked' with his brother and a friend. Our original policeman and policewoman had sent for back-up and three other police cars and six men had come; they were discreetly waiting in the car park near the men's car until the men returned, which they did.

One opened up the car door and one got in the back with the trolley, then the police pounced and all hell was let loose. They ran; the police ran. Shoppers stood and stared. Eventually the policewoman caught one, and another was caught, but one got away. The two were handcuffed and taken to the police station. Sally went in one car and I went in another, and for an hour we toured the city but we could not find the man in the beautiful grey shirt and trousers. (I hoped he ruined them with sweat.)

We were dropped off at our shop by the police officers and we felt so deflated. The police were now in charge. I think I took Sally home in my car and then went home myself. I was exhausted.

Next morning at the shop we received a visit from a detective constable I had spoken to about our three men on the previous day. His visit started the butterflies roaring around inside Sally and me. You see, because we had not actually physically stopped the three men it might be suggested that the police had stopped the wrong men. Even though they had opened the car door and were getting in as the police approached them, maybe they were not the shoplifters I had seen but just three men stealing their car, even though they were wearing clothes matching the description I had given to the police.

The upshot was that Sally and I were to visit the police station at noon for an identity parade. Although I had been doing this job for about twelve years never before had I done an identity parade. I was feeling decidedly ill. I seem to remember the hours slowly passing between many cups of coffee until at eleven fifty-five we presented ourselves at police headquarters. Panic: Sally and I should not have been together! I was quickly bustled into a small back office on my own and told not to move until told, and Sally was taken elsewhere. I sat and sat and sat and sat.

An hour and ten minutes later a young man came into the office, looked at me, said "Blast!" and walked out again.

After a further twenty minutes my original detective constable came in and said, "I'm ever so sorry, but one of the men insists on having his solicitor and I cannot get hold of him. I've told the canteen to keep some dinner for Sally and you. I'm sorry you've got to be kept apart, but, you see, you cannot discuss the case as you are both witnesses."

A further hour passed and then, feeling quite faint, I heard someone coming along the corridor and a friendly police officer said, "Mrs Smith?"

I nodded.

He continued: "Please follow close behind me and speak to no one."

We went down a long corridor. Was I the accused? I wondered – I certainly felt as though I was being treated like the villain. We came to a lift. A young constable was holding it for us. I wanted to run, but all around I appeared to be guarded by policemen. There were no smiles, no jokes. Had they got the wrong person? Anyway, down I went in the lift with a policeman on either side of me. Would one of them put the handcuffs on me? We don't have the electric chair in this country, do we? The lift bumped to a stop and jolted my thoughts back to reality.

As I stepped out of the lift another policeman spoke to my two guards: "Has she spoken to anyone?"

They shook their heads.

Hurrah – here was my detective constable!

He said, "Don't look so nervous."

I stuttered, "I'm petrified!"

He put his arm round my shoulders and I felt a bit better. We stood for a few seconds and then a door that I was facing opened and I was signalled to enter. My legs took over; my brain had stopped functioning. I entered and saw eleven young men all the same height, all with grey/black hair, all with moustaches, all standing in a row. All had their hands behind their backs. My God!

A policeman at a sort of desk said, "Madam, yesterday a man or men were involved in stealing a record deck from one shop and a radio/cassette player from another in this city. If you see one or any of these men here today, would you touch him or them on the right shoulder, please. Now walk along the line of men."

So it was a record deck they had stolen from my shop – the

probable value was about £200. I mustn't make a mistake. They all looked alike. 'Number 1, no; Number 2, don't know . . . Stop, woman – control yourself. Place yourself in the shop and remember the face of the man who took the radio/cassette player from the window. Number 3, no; Number 4, no; Number 5, *yes*.'

It was him. Before I could think my hand shot out and touched his right shoulder.

There was one other sign from this young man that helped me decide it was him, and long afterwards when Sally and I were discussing the ordeal we both agreed it was a sign of his guilt. However, I cannot disclose here what it was because again later we learnt that it is often this small thing that helps police officers to pick out a suspect. We knew nothing of this beforehand, and I must say here and now that although we were friendly with the police and they would often help us, in no way did they give us a clue about anything that would help us to pick out the villains.

Now back to the line-up. The police officer at the desk said, "Thank you," and I continued along the line, but the two other men weren't there.

I walked back to the desk, and then I noticed that a solicitor was making notes and four other police officers were in the room. My arm was touched by my guard police officer and he ushered me out of another door. We went round a corner into another lift. Again this was being held by a young constable.

We got in and my police guard said, "It wasn't too bad, was it?"

I said, "Ghastly."

We arrived in another office and I was again left to wait. I wished I smoked.

The policewoman came in and said, "Are you OK? You looked awful downstairs."

All I could say was "Never again!"

She roared with laughter and said, "You do know you've got another one in about half an hour."

I was stunned.

"Yes," she said. "The two fellows we got yesterday are so unlike each other that we need another line-up."

I gave up and just quietly waited.

I was again collected. I retraced my steps with my guards. I entered the room. I was now in complete charge of myself. I was not panicking, but perhaps I should have been. Which one was it? There was no sign, as there had been with the first man. They all looked as if they might have done it. I walked up and down the line. Was it Number 7 or Number 8? Number 7 was very like him, but there was also something about Number 8. His eyes were the eyes I'd seen looking around in the shop, but this man had a scar down the side of his face. My man didn't, or did he? Had it been covered by his hair? Oh dear, oh dear! Number 7 or Number 8? I stopped and shut my eyes and tried to picture the man in the shop. Yes, Number 8 had the right eyes – but that scar, why hadn't I seen it yesterday? Why? Who? Why? Who? Was it Number 7? His eyes were not quite right, but everything else was. He had no scar, and I didn't remember a scar. No, it *was* Number 8. I touched him on the shoulder and then I was taken out.

Ten minutes later I had to sign a statement relating to the identity parade. My detective constable was very quiet and I felt dreadful. I began to think I'd picked the wrong one. I felt sure about the first one, but I thought I must have boobed on the second. Sally then joined me.

The Detective Constable came back and said, "Thank you, ladies."

We said, "For goodness' sake, what happened?"

"Well," he said, "Mrs Smith, many, many thanks." Sally got just one 'many thanks'. Sally had picked the wrong brown-haired man.

She said, "I knew as soon as I came out that it should have been the man with the scar, but I don't remember seeing it yesterday."

The time was now four o'clock and we'd had no dinner. We went home.

Two days passed and then the Detective Constable contacted us again and said, "At 3 p.m. today we are holding an ID parade for your third man. We've picked him up near his home town."

Oh no – not all that performance again! I feared the man might have drastically changed his appearance. If the moustache was gone and he'd dyed his hair, I would be lost. There was no hint from the police. We went to the police station and again were separated. This time everything went to plan and was over quite quickly.

I was again taken downstairs in the lift, and confronted by eleven men, all alike. I saw him as I entered. I tried to look at the others, but no, he was the one. His moustache was still there, and his hair was the same as I'd seen it three days earlier. Even as he stood in the line-up and I knew he was a villain I still fancied him. As I put my hand forward to touch him on the shoulder, he bent towards me and winked, the saucy devil. Later I learnt from Sally that when she put her hand out to touch his shoulder he grabbed her hand and plonked it on his shoulder. He was nice. About six months later the two brothers (the other two men) pleaded guilty to shoplifting at our Crown Court. The first man was fined £300 and got twelve months inside; the second man got eighteen months inside and a fine of £150.

The last man told the police he didn't know what his friends had been doing. He came to the Crown Court three weeks later and pleaded not guilty. When the police had first spoken to him he had said he'd come to our city for a swim. How logical! He came fifty miles from the seaside, where there were many swimming pools, to our city with its very poor swimming facilities, without his swimming costume or even a towel! Sally and I were told to attend the Crown Court, which we did.

Crown Courts, of course, are presided over by a judge, and twelve good and true men or women sit on the jury. Our brown-haired man was in the dock and several of his friends were in court as company for him.

I was the first to go into the witness box and I was questioned by a rather fat man in a curly wig and long black robe. I was asked which way I followed the men around town. I described the route they took.

The judge looked over the edge of his balcony and said, "You didn't mention going past Woolworth's."

I replied, "Because we didn't."

The judge said, "Of course you did, or else how could you have got to the music shop?"

I said, "We didn't go past Woolworth's because we went up — Lane, which bypasses Woolworth's."

The judge rearranged his robes and sat back – a little disgruntled, I felt. More questions were asked, and I answered until I said the man looked around.

The judge shot forward in his seat and bellowed, "Did you say looked round or around?"

I replied with a slight shrug of my shoulders, "Around."

He looked at me quite fiercely and said, "Pay attention. Did you say he looked *a round* or he looked *round*?"

I repeated, "Around."

No more was said. My questions finished and I left the courtroom.

Sally said her bit and, thankfully, we left the courthouse. The hearing was to go on, because unbeknown to us other charges were being put to the young man. We breathed a sigh of relief – we thought it was all over.

Oh, no, it wasn't. Two days later we heard that there had to be a retrial with the same judge but a different jury. Someone had let it slip in court that the man had been in trouble with the police before, and a jury must have no idea before they reach a verdict if the accused is a villain or not. A new date was fixed for three weeks later.

I went into the box, and after I had given my evidence the judge leant forward and said, "Madam, you did not go past Woolworth's, did you?" He had such a twinkle in his eye!

Later in my evidence I said, "The man looked around him." I looked at the judge, and again his eyes twinkled and the corners of his mouth turned up.

All, this time, proceeded properly and a verdict of guilty was brought in. The young man got twelve months in prison.

As you know, the item stolen from my shop was a record deck. After being at the police station it was returned to the shop. It was returned to the electrical department and again it went on show. Three weeks later the stylus was stolen from it. For a further six weeks it stood in the warehouse until a new stylus was purchased and fitted. It again went out on display. It was decided to reduce the price because of its history and length of stay in various places. A new assistant was taken on in the department and we forgot the deck until one day I saw it had gone. Hurrah! It had been sold.

In the course of conversation I found out that the new assistant had paid £30 because he had heard it was being reduced and had taken it home. Another crime had been committed. No one had given authority to reduce the price from £300 to £30 – after all, the shop had just paid £20 for a new stylus. The manager was mad. He dismissed the assistant and the record deck was returned to the shop, and there it continued to sit. Every time I saw it I wondered who would be the next unfortunate to want it.

Now a few words about child shoplifters. A child under the age of ten is below the age of criminal responsibility; so, as shoplifting is a criminal offence, no prosecutions ensue from children under ten being caught. However, this does not mean children don't do it.

One afternoon I was in a food shop and the time was about four o'clock. Nothing much was happening and I was preparing to go home. I gathered together a few items – a frozen chicken and other goodies for dinner. I was just going to the checkout when I noticed a girl of about nine years standing in front of the sweet displays. She had with her a carrier bag containing something. It was a lovely sunny warm day, so she had no coat. She was looking around her and I had a decidedly itchy feeling. The frozen chicken was beginning to burn my arm. I grabbed an assistant and she replaced my frozen chicken in the fridge and I continued to watch the very young lady. She moved away from the sweets and along to the cake displays. She walked up and down looking at the cake. She kept returning to a box of chocolate slices. She stood in front of them. She put her bag on the floor. A customer walked past, and she moved away. The aisle was empty except for the girl. I was peering through a fixture. The girl picked up the box of chocolate slices, but another customer came round the corner. She literally threw the slices into the fixture. She picked up her bag and walked up and down and up and down. Again the aisle cleared. She rushed up to the slices, grabbed them, shoved them into her own bag and was away up to the top of the shop.

She slowed as she went past the checkout, which gave me time to catch up. Together we went through the outside doors.

I grabbed her arm and said, "You didn't pay for the slices, did you?"

She was amazed. After a short silence she said, "How do you know?"

I said, "I'm the store detective and you are coming back to the manager with me."

She started hollering and shouting: "I'm not, I'm not."

I said, "Now, be quiet because everyone is looking at you." I had to shut her up somehow because people were beginning to look at me as if I was trying to molest the child.

Anyway, we returned to the office.

As we entered, the manager looked at me and said, "A big time crook here, eh?" and we grinned.

I told the manager of the circumstances, and he said to the girl, "Shall I call for a policeman to lock you up, or will you go quietly with this lady who's going to see your mum?"

"No!" screamed the girl. "I've only just been let out. My mum kept me in for a week for pinchin' her fags. I don't wanna be locked in again."

"Well," said the manager, "what about going to prison? That's worse."

The girl said, "OK, I'll go with her."

The manager said, "Now, don't give the lady any trouble. She's karate-trained and has bionic legs."

The girl looked at me in awe. After all, she still didn't know how I'd seen her pinch the slices.

We went to my car and got in. She'd given me her address, so I knew roughly where she lived. Then off we went.

The policy of my firm is that the store detective takes the youngsters they catch home, because often we found that the little blighters would give a false name and address.

We arrived and I knocked on the door. The child was sobbing and crying.

Her father opened the door, looked daggers at me and said, "What's the matter?" and said the child's name.

The child said, "Oh, Dad!" and rushed past him into the house.

Her father bristled and I hastily showed him my identity card and said, "Your daughter stole from my shop."

The father reeled round and said to the fleeing daughter, "You little b—! I'll — thrash the daylights out of you."

From the back a voice called, "What the bloody hell is going on?"

The father yelled, "The —'s done it again. She's been bloody shoplifting."

The owner of the voice appeared and it was the girl's mother.

She cuffed the daughter across the ears and then, seeing me, she said, "Oh."

She looked at the father and he said, "She's the store detective."

The mother regained her composure and said, "Well, don't leave her on the step. Ask her in."

The door was held open and in I went. We went into an exceedingly grubby kitchen/diner. Unwashed dishes still surrounded the portable TV on the table. A saucer was full of fag ends. There were cups without saucers everywhere. The ceiling over the cooker was hanging in brown flakes and cobwebs. The draining board by the sink contained a few empty whisky and gin bottles. A large mongrel dog leapt all over me as I stood waiting for a bit of hush! The mother was yelling at her daughter, who was sobbing and yelling – but no tears!

The mother noticed that the window was open. "Shut that bloody window!" she said to the girl's father. "All the — neighbours will hear. Oh," she said, turning to me, "I'm sorry, but we've had so much trouble with her. She's only just been allowed out because she and her friends pinched my fags last week." That seemed to remind her of something. She turned to her daughter and said, "I suppose you were with them. I've told you not to go with them." She turned to me and said, "It's them – they make her bad."

I then got a word in and said, "Well, it's my firm's policy to return child shoplifters to their homes and not call the police the first time, but should she do it again it will be reported to them."

The girl's parents both said, "Thank you very much," and out I went.

I drove straight home as it was now five fifteen, and I went to cook the dinner – no chicken; fish and chips again.

Another incident involving children actually happened in the same shop.

The manager phoned me at my office and said, "The headmaster of one of our local schools has a boy of six years of age 'doing' the local shops. Last night he took several items from our shop and sold them in school today."

The headmaster had informed the police, but they could do nothing. After all, he might have come by the items legitimately. The headmaster had informed the manager, who told me that the boy was about three feet six inches tall, with fair hair; he wore a green anorak which was at least two sizes too big and a pair of maroon trousers with big turn-ups. He usually carried his shoe bag, and that was probably where he would put his loot. He would leave school at three thirty and would be at the shop about five minutes later.

I arrived and waited. Promptly at three thirty-five a tiny figure wearing a too large anorak and too long maroon trousers turned up, carrying a shoe bag, was observing all the goings-on inside our shop from outside. As the manager walked past the window the tiny figure moved away, and as the manager went out of sight the tiny figure reappeared. He was looking so hard. He was a true professional shoplifter. Sometimes our shop managers are too eager, and this was the case now. The boy wouldn't enter the shop until the manager was out of the way. It was no skin off his nose if he had to wait, he might have said. He took one more look. The manager was still hanging about, so off he went up the road.

He didn't know about me, so I followed him. He went past the post office and, after a quick recce through the window, he entered a shop. It was wintertime so it was dark outside.

I stood outside the window and looked through. Inside, he stood looking around him. He loosened the strings on his shoe bag and approached a display. His hand moved up and back and the shoe bag was closed. I was watching and saw nothing, but I knew he'd got something. He sort of smirked. He looked around. His hand went out and a box of hankies went under his jacket. There were customers around, but nobody seemed to notice. He was looking around him and walking towards the exit doors.

As he came out I grabbed him by the scruff of the neck and, holding very tightly, I said, "You've just pinched some things."

He started screaming and wriggling. "No, I ain't, missus," he said.

His boots were now being aimed at my legs so my grip on the back of his shirt started to twist and he realized that I meant business. I started to drag him into the shop. I think some of the customers must have thought what a dreadful mother I was because they started to look and point.

With this wriggling tiny person I approached an assistant and said, "Can I see your manager?" Remember, I was not in one of my own shops so no one knew who I was.

The assistant, perhaps trying to protect the manager, said, "I'm sorry, but he's busy."

My young friend had by now kicked me twice and I was smarting. I was unable to release my hold on the boy to get out my identity card or he would have gone, so I marched straight past the assistant to the back of the shop, shoving the boy before me and the assistant out of the way.

Of course this made them get the manager, and when I had explained who I was and what had happened we went into the office. I took a key ring from the shoe bag and the box of hankies from under the boy's coat.

I asked the manager to call the police, as the headmaster had asked we should if we caught him.

As the manager phoned from the office the boy said, "It won't do no good, mister. They can't do nothing – I'm too young."

He took some sweets from his pocket and started to suck them noisily.

The police arrived and said to me, "Hey, you're in the wrong shop," and laughed. Then they saw the boy. "You again!" one of them said, and the child said, "Yeah, what you gonna do about it?"

One of the police officers said to me, "That's the trouble: there is nothing we can do except take him home. By the way, his dad's a right villain."

Little did I think that two years later, unbeknown to me, I did catch the boy's father – in the same shop.

The policeman said to me, "How did you manage to catch him? He usually runs like the wind and – no offence – can you run like that?"

"Ha ha!" I said. "I grabbed his collar before I spoke to him."

The officer said, "Well, you know how to deal with them after a few years, don't you?"

Anyway, they drove the boy home.

FIRST AID

We (Sally, Janet and I) were getting rather disturbed at our inability to deal with fainting shoplifters, and our biggest dread was stopping an elderly person who then had a heart attack or someone who flew into an epileptic fit, either genuine or put on.

Janet and I were at a large food store and Janet was grabbed by the manager and taken to the staff toilets. There on the floor was a dead assistant, a young girl. Janet felt powerless to do anything. She had never even seen a dead person, let alone a staff member we had been speaking to less than half an hour previously. Janet called for me, and the manager sent for a doctor, who arrived in seconds. I arrived just after the ambulance got there, so fortunately I was not involved except to drive the staff member's boyfriend home. He was in a state of shock.

All the other staff members had a sweet cup of tea to try to relieve the shock. It really was awful. We were struggling to cope. We had heard of artificial respiration, but knew nothing about how to apply it. We seriously wondered if we could have saved the young girl's life.

We were upset and discussed going on a first-aid course; but things slide away, and two weeks later Sally had to deal with a similarly unpleasant episode.

For many weeks Sally had noticed a very large lady with her husband and a child in a pushchair spending a long time in one of our stores. Sally wondered if they were shoplifting, but had never seen anything to suggest that they were.

One afternoon Sally was called by the manager. The husband had gone to the manager and told him that his wife had gone into the ladies' toilet about half an hour previously and he was worried. Sally accompanied the manager to the ladies' toilet and found the very large lady dead on the floor. Again a very nasty shock! Sally felt useless. I must put in here that in both cases (the young lady staff member and the large lady) death was inevitable. They both had heart trouble, so we could have done nothing to help, but we still felt inadequate.

On another occasion I was questioning a staff member about thefts from her till. She said, "If you don't leave me alone I'll have an epileptic fit."

I soft-pedalled, just in case.

When her case came to court she did throw a fit when she heard the magistrate pronounce her guilty. The court was able to produce a police surgeon, for which I was very grateful. He found it was a sham fit, but I would not have known.

Fits and minor faints, dizziness, muzziness and other excuses tended to worry us, so I went to our staff training officer and asked if we could please go on a first-aid course.

Nine months later we did – not through neglect on the part of the staff trainer, but owing to the fact that courses were so busy and booked up months ahead (nine, in our case). Two days before we were due to attend, I was sent for by my chief. Although I had previously discussed it with him it had not sunk in, so he suddenly realized that his security team, all of it, was to be away for four whole days. You'd have thought the place was about to fall apart, whereas we'd always thought the firm found us a bit of a nuisance, always poking our noses into other people's business. However, I managed to convince my chief that September, which it was then, was a quiet month; and I said that should the course finish early any day, we would rush to our shops to protect them. So we were allowed to go.

Monday morning saw us bright-eyed and bushy-tailed. We arrived, parked our cars and in we went. About forty others joined us – men and women from all sorts of work. There were teachers, factory hands, firemen, office workers, three young ladies from our local newspaper and many others we never spoke to.

The instructor started to speak when we were all settled in our chairs. More or less the first thing she said after introducing herself was "and Thursday afternoon will be entirely devoted to the exam by the visiting doctors".

A gasp went up. An exam – no way had we expected that! It was twenty-four years since I left school, and apart from passing my driving test I had gone completely soft in the head. How would I manage? If Janet and Sally had not been with me, I would not have returned on the Monday afternoon. Later I found out from them that had I not been there they would have chickened out. Anyway, we were all issued with the first-aid manual – all 201 pages of it – containing details of what to do in the event of heart attacks, epileptic fits, sprains and strains, strokes . . . In fact, it contained everything anyone would expect to find in a first-aid manual, including 'Bleeding, How to Stop It' and 'Resuscitation'.

We were introduced to Resusci Anne, the top half of a body – a plastic one, let me say. There was a head and face, with a movable lower jaw. The neck also moved and the breastbone was there, and underneath were two flat bags pretending to be lungs. There was the heart, from which came two transparent plastic tubes, one with red liquid and one with blue liquid. We were shown resuscitation. One lady demonstrator placed Resusci Anne on a blanket on the floor, then knelt down, pulled the dummy's head up, pushed her fingers into the dummy's mouth and fished out a set of false teeth. The lady then proceeded to place her mouth over the dummy's mouth and blow. The 'lungs' inflated and deflated beautifully. We were then told we would 'have a go' during the afternoon.

I was petrified. I've got some false teeth and I could just imagine them being blown into the dummy's mouth. I had for a long time been intending to go to the dentist to have them refitted as they were a bit loose. Why did I always leave things?

A doctor lectured us for one and a half hours, then we went for coffee. We returned to another hour session of lectures from the doctor. He was young and so nice. Why couldn't my own doctor be like him? The lecture doctor had us in fits of laughter. He answered any questions and waited until we really understood. He seemed interested in each of us.

We had lunch. All our talk was about the exam. The three of us were joined at our table by an older man, who said his wife and daughter had passed the exam so he really felt he must too. He was a Scoutmaster and we heard all his troubles.

The other person at our table was a woman who had to travel twenty miles by bus to get to the lectures. She was a divorcee and she said the extra money her firm would pay her if she passed her exam would help her financial state. What extra money? Sally, Janet and I wished to hear more. Well, it appeared that a qualified first-aider should receive an extra payment of about £1 per week; but it was at the discretion of the firm, so I'll say no more.

The afternoons were to be devoted to learning how to bandage hurt people, so we paired up. Sally was with me; Janet was with the lady with the extra money if she passed; and the man was with another man, who turned out to be a security officer in a factory. He was a nice man. We were all handed triangular bandages and shown how to fold them properly, and then the fun started. We ladies were advised to wear trousers for the next day, but that day we did just arm and above-the-waist bandaging.

Sally and I are by no means Twiggy types – more your Diana Dors – and the bandages for broken arms which are strapped to the body were not large enough. This caused much laughter as we were trying to bandage each other. One bandage I was using on Sally (I forget what for) ended up with two ends to tie at her front. One of the demonstrators took me aside and suggested I took the ends to the back of Sally because, as it was, there was nowhere to tie the knot. We did laugh. We tried resuscitation and my fears of lost teeth were not justified. Then it was cup-of-tea time and an hour later found us ready to leave for home with instructions to learn the manual and try bandaging the family.

We went home shattered. We really felt we had been put through the mangle.

I got our evening meal at home, and my sons, when they learnt I wanted to practise bandaging, suddenly found important appointments that could not be avoided. This left Ron. We landed up on the kitchen floor and, with his help, I succeeded fairly well in immobilizing most parts of him, which was the whole object of the exercise.

I didn't sleep at all well that night, but returned to the lectures on Tuesday. We continued learning bandaging and trying out the resuscitation with the dummy until Thursday lunchtime. By now everyone was in a right tizz. We'd all learnt so much that we knew nothing. Questions flew about.

"What do you do for a heart attack?"

"I don't know; what *do* you do for a heart attack?"

"I don't know – that's why I asked you."

It sounded like a comedy routine. Fingers flew through pages of the manual.

"Ah, yes," – mumble, mumble – "I thought that was a fit."

We scratched at our dinners. Someone dropped a glass. It was cleared up. We were given a number for the order in which we would take the exam. We had to go in turns to the two doctors for an oral test and then to a first-aider to do a bandage test and then a resuscitation test.

I was 17, Sally was 18 and Janet 19 – not first, not last. And so we waited. As 1, 2 and 3 came out we all asked, "How was it?"

"Fine," they said, but they all looked stunned.

They were given a cup of tea, and so it went on until 17 was called.

In I went. A very nice elderly gentleman doctor asked me a few questions. I knew the answers.

He said, "What job do you do?"

I said, "I'm a store detective."

"Oh!" he said. "I'll look out for you in shops."

I continued and did my bandaging and then went on to Resusci Anne. That was OK. Out I went and got my cup of tea. Sally followed close behind me. We thankfully sat down with our tea.

Sally said, "I've laddered my tights."

I looked down and saw that blood was running from her knee, down her leg and dripping on to the floor. Panic! What to do? Everyone was flapping about.

Eventually one of the first-aid demonstrators came in because of the noise we were all making. She quickly got the first-aid box and attended to Sally's knee. By now we were all laughing. Not one of us would pass our exam – our very first emergency and we'd all gone up the wall! Then I began to wonder how Sally could have cut her knee. Sally told us that as she knelt to do the resuscitation she felt a prick, and then someone remembered a glass that had been broken at lunchtime. The exam was halted and a piece of glass was found near a small pool of Sally's blood. Off went the exams again for those numbered after us. We went home.

Two weeks later there was great excitement. Our firm received our certificates and badges. The firm was amazed – three passes out of three entrants. Wonderful! Our publicity manager wanted to put our photographs in the staff magazine, but I said no. After all, we were not supposed to be known to the staff and customers. If a shoplifter got hold of our pictures, they'd know who we were; so a small piece was printed saying, 'Our security staff are now qualified first-aiders so any problem in your shops can be dealt with by them.' We were also presented with a gift of £10 each as a token of appreciation from the firm.

Sally, Janet and I learnt one important thing on that course: to run in the opposite direction should we come across an accident. We were more terrified with our knowledge than without it.

For about four months we managed to be just too late for accidents that occurred in the shops, or else there was another qualified first-aider on hand in the particular shop.

Just after Christmas, over the Tannoy system in one of our larger shop came "Would the first-aid lady come to the fashion floor? Thank you."

I nearly fainted. Sally and Janet were to join me in about half an hour – I was early.

Over the Tannoy: "Would the manager come to the fashion floor?"

My mind was in a turmoil. My legs were like jelly. I'd be no good – surely someone else would go.

An assistant from the fashion floor arrived in the menswear department and went to a woman assistant. "Come quick," she said. "We haven't got a first-aider and you know a bit."

I shook myself and ran upstairs to the fashion floor. There, lying on the floor surrounded by curious customers, was a very large gentleman. He was about seventy-five years old. He was conscious. Someone – perhaps even he – had removed his false teeth. The assistant from the menswear department was frantically going through the man's pockets. She undid his trousers belt. I think he thought he was in for trouble because he started grabbing at her hands.

I could see he was getting distressed, so I said, "Hey, go easy."

She replied, "He might have a bad heart and I'm looking for tablets or a talisman, but I can't find anything."

I replied, "Take it easy."

She said, "Are you a first-aider?"

I said, "Yes."

She said, "You get on with it. I can't find anything," and off she went.

By now my legs had given way, so I was on the floor beside the man. I took his hand in mine to reassure him and to take his pulse – no way could I find it, but it looked professional.

I then said, "What happened?"

The man touched his head and made circular movements with his hand.

I said, "You were dizzy?"

He looked blank. A bystander said the man had fallen all the way down the stairs. The man started moving his tongue about so I sent someone for some water. By now the man had gone to his pocket and taken out his glasses in a case. He put them on. Still lying on the floor, he handed me a piece of paper taken from his glasses case. It gave his address. The water came and the man obviously wanted to sit up, so the manager and I propped him up on the bottom step. He had a sip of water and then put his teeth back in and his hat on top of his head. He then took a pen from his pocket and also a small pad. He wrote his name.

I replied on the paper with 'AMBULANCE IS COMING.'

He nodded.

Then I wrote, 'FAMILY'.

He wrote the word 'daughter' and gave us a phone number on the paper.

With that, up came the ambulance men and Sally.

She said, "I thought you'd got a shoplifter and he'd passed out."

Janet found us and we went for coffee. I was drained. The daughter was phoned and advised of the situation. The ambulance men said they had dealt with him before.

I thanked God for supporting me through my first first-aid problem. I was glad it was not too serious and that I coped fairly well. Please, shoplifters, should I catch you, don't have a heart attack – I'd race you to the Pearly Gates.

SOMEONE YOU KNOW

In my fifteenth year as a store detective I was still getting surprises. We had a very busy pre-Christmas period, and I caught many shoplifters, all with a lot of stolen goodies. I was tired. On 23 December I visited our largest store, which was the one nearest to home. The shop was fairly busy. Lots of children were visiting Father Christmas, who sat on the ground floor on a red throne surrounded by toys. Beside him was a big tub of packets of sweets, which he gave free to children. Yes, in the late 1970s sweets were given free to children who stopped and spoke to Santa.

    I stood watching. My children were grown-up. As he spoke to the children I watched the wonder in their faces. It took me back many years. How quickly they grow up! He was a lovely Father Christmas, kind and happy. All the children took to him. I felt a little sad. Most of my life was now so businesslike, and there was little magic in Christmas for me any more. I'd bought a new suit for one son, and money for the other. There would be no lovely parcels under our tree, no excitement. I thought of all those years when it had been difficult money-wise to get what the children wanted, but we'd managed and had fun repainting second-hand bikes and doing up parcels for Father Christmas to deliver. I moved away, thinking I must be getting broody and was wanting to be a grandmother.

    About half an hour later I wandered through the perfumery department. All was very quiet. Father Christmas was in the department looking at boxes of perfume. I came back to earth with a bump. I knew he was going to pinch them. He picked up two boxes, slid them up inside his jacket and readjusted his wide black belt. I couldn't believe it. I was rooted to the spot, but I'd seen it.

The manager walked past me, so I grabbed him and told him what I'd seen.

He replied, "There's bells on his sleigh, so pull the other one," but then he looked at my face and knew I meant it.

We both just stood there. Eventually he walked away.

I continued to watch Father Christmas as other items went up inside his jacket. I felt sick.

Off he went to the staffroom as it was his lunch break. He changed and came out at the rear of the shop. I stopped him. Yes, he had several items with him that he had not paid for. The police were called.

When two officers arrived they were grinning all over their faces. I wondered why, but learnt later that over the car radio the two police officers had been called to our shop with the words "Father Christmas has been caught shoplifting."

They were most disappointed that he was an ordinary man out of his garb, in a raincoat and cap. Anyway, they all went to the police station, and as Father Christmas was an elderly person of previous good character he was cautioned.

In the pre-Christmas spirit the police sergeant said, "As you have a very busy night tomorrow over the rooftops we are cautioning you this time."

Of course word spread throughout our store: "Father Christmas has been nicked pinching."

Unfortunately he was unable to return to his position in the afternoon and several kiddies were disappointed. Many of the staff who still felt the magic of Christmas were disgusted with me. Fancy catching Father Christmas!

IN CONCLUSION

If you are a person tempted to try shoplifting, or, indeed, if you are doing that very thing in your local shops now, have you ever stopped and wondered what will happen if you are caught? Oh, I see – you are not going to get caught. Well, maybe not tomorrow, but when? Because it will happen! Perhaps today an assistant noticed you. Oh, of course you were very careful. No one saw. But that assistant saw you place a tin of salmon in your basket and it was not presented at the checkout. No action was taken today, but the assistant will have informed the manager, and next time he will either watch you himself or call in the shop security people – ordinary 'nothing' people, like me.

They will be watching you when you start your shopping, carrying your shopping bag and the wire basket. You will start to wander around, and in will go a box of Weetabix, two half-pound packets of butter, two packets of tea, a two-pound bag of sugar. All quite safely go into your basket. You will bend down in a corner of the shop, and as you straighten up you will have your back to me. I will look into the basket you are carrying, and I'll notice there is no tea and no butter. You will look around you and off you will go to the checkout to pay for your Weetabix and sugar.

You will chat in a most friendly way to the checkout girl: "What awful weather! Yes, we had a lovely holiday. We went to Devon," etc., etc., but I will notice your neck is bouncing up and down with the quickness of your pulse.

Do you honestly think that will do you any good?

Anyway, you will collect your change and out you'll go. Outside the shop I will approach.

"Excuse me, madam. I am a security officer and you have just left the shop with some butter and tea you did not pay for."

Never in all my life have I had anyone stop me, but I wonder how it must feel. The shoplifter must have thought she'd got away with it or she'd never have left the shop, but then she (or you) had done it so often before and never been seen.

I will try to keep you as calm as possible. I don't want a scene outside on the pavement, so I will say, "Please come back to the manager's office with me."

"No, no," you will say, "I'm not coming in there. You just take it back."

I will say, "Look, dear – if you start making a fuss, everyone will know what you've done. Just come back inside and we'll discuss it."

People by now will be beginning to look, so I will hurry you inside.

It will probably have dawned on you by now that you have been caught stealing. It may sound less serious to call it shoplifting, but in actual fact the thing you have done is stealing – yes, stealing. If I left my purse on my kitchen table at home and you were in my house, you would not take it – but then, you are not a thief. You only go shoplifting – everyone does it nowadays. Oh, yes! But when you are caught it turns out that that 'harmless' shoplifting episode is a criminal offence. It is stealing.

You will now start to realize what is happening. The police will arrive and I shall tell them what you've done. They will ask you if you have anything to say, but by this time your mouth may be too dry to speak.

A lot of women do say, "Please don't tell my husband – don't put it in the paper."

The police try to park discreetly at the back of the shop, but sometimes that is not possible and you may have to walk through the shop with two burly police officers, and you will have to get into a panda car. And if the panda car only has two doors there will be a very undignified scramble into the back.

The public love to have a look. In their eyes anyone in the back of a panda car is probably a serious criminal. Mind you, I often wonder whether, as they watch the proceedings, any of them have got unpaid-for items in their bags. Perhaps they will think they are more clever than the shoplifter who has been caught; but then, that's what you all think.

You will arrive at the police station, and on the way you will have heard the officer speaking on his radio: "I'm now bringing in a prisoner." Yes, *you*.

The back door at the police station is manned. You will scramble out of the car and enter the building. The door will be locked behind you. You will sit on a bench while a sergeant will hear what has happened from the police officer who brought you in.

Of course the exact procedure varies from police area to police area, but your belongings will be searched and maybe you will even be subjected to a body search. This will be done by a policewoman if you are female. Your photograph may be taken at this stage; likewise your fingerprints may be taken and printed on a card. Maybe your home will be searched. Imagine the neighbours if a police car turns up at your house! The police may ask your husband to come to the police station to collect you, because by now you will probably be in a state.

You may say, "Why all the fuss? It was only butter and tea," but the fact is you are a criminal, a person who stole.

You will probably be released to go home, and then in most cases a court summons will duly arrive by recorded delivery.

My son had a smooth tyre on his car and was caught and was sent a court summons by recorded delivery.

The postman knocked on my door and handed it to me and said, "Doesn't look too healthy, does it?" and grinned. Across the brown envelope was printed the name of my local constabulary. I signed and groaned, but it was for my son. How will you feel if one is delivered to your door, for you?

The date for your appearance will come round and off you will go. You will be instructed to be at the magistrates' court at 10 a.m. When you arrive you will be confronted by criminals – drug addicts, thugs and thieves – oh yes, but you too are a thief. Remember, you stole.

You may have to wait for a couple of hours because everyone

has to be there at ten o'clock, but eventually the court usher shouts your name and in you will go. You will stand in the dock and face the magistrates.

The chairman will say, "What do you plead?" after the prosecution has read out the charge.

If you say, "Guilty," the case will continue and at the end you will find out your punishment – a fine, a conditional discharge, community service or whatever the magistrates decide – and you will leave the court. If you decide to say you are not guilty, another date will be set for your appearance. I will be there then to say what I saw; so will the policeman who took you to the police station.

After reading this, do you still think it is worthwhile shoplifting, or STEALING? No matter what I've said, the professional or couldn't-care-less, society-owes-me-a-living type will laugh at me and say they make a good living at shoplifting. Perhaps they will spend a couple of months inside if caught – that to them is a change.

The person I want to urge not to steal is the ordinary nice person – my neighbour, your neighbour – who might think it's easy and get tempted.

DON'T.